Eve
Isn't
Evil

Eve Isn't Evil

Feminist Readings of the Bible
to Upend Our Assumptions

Julie Faith Parker

Baker Academic
a division of Baker Publishing Group
Grand Rapids, Michigan

© 2023 by Julie Faith Parker

Published by Baker Academic
a division of Baker Publishing Group
Grand Rapids, Michigan
www.bakeracademic.com

Printed in the United States of America

Library of Congress Cataloging-in-Publication Data
Names: Parker, Julie F., author.
Title: Eve isn't evil : feminist readings of the Bible to upend our assumptions / Julie
    Faith Parker.
Description: Grand Rapids, Michigan : Baker Academic, a division of Baker Publishing
    Group, [2023]
Identifiers: LCCN 2022059991 | ISBN 9781540965394 (paperback) | ISBN
    9781540966872 (casebound) | ISBN 9781493443000 (ebook) | ISBN 9781493443017
    (pdf)
Subjects: LCSH: Bible. Old Testament—Feminist criticism. | Eve (Biblical figure) |
    Feminist theology. | Women in the Bible. | Women—Conduct of life—Anecdotes.
Classification: LCC BS1181.8 .P36 2023 | DDC 221.6—dc23/eng/20230526
LC record available at https://lccn.loc.gov/2022059991)

Ansel Elkins, "Autobiography of Eve." In *Blue Yodel*. New Haven: Yale University Press, 2015. Used by permission.

Baker Publishing Group publications use paper produced from sustainable forestry practices and post-consumer waste whenever possible.

23   24   25   26   27   28   29   7   6   5   4   3   2   1

to Graham and Mari

עצם מעצמי ובשר מבשרי
"bone of my bones, and flesh of my flesh"
Genesis 2:23a

I love you
forever

Autobiography of Eve

Wearing nothing but snakeskin
boots, I blazed a footpath, the first
radical road out of that old kingdom
toward a new unknown.
When I came to those great flaming gates
of burning gold,
I stood alone in terror at the threshold
between Paradise and Earth.
There I heard a mysterious echo:
my own voice
singing to me from across the forbidden
side. I shook awake—
at once alive in a blaze of green fire.

Let it be known: I did not fall from grace.

I leapt
to freedom.

—*Ansel Elkins*

Contents

In the Beginning . . .

The genesis of this book was a meeting with a medium. A chance opportunity in the spring of 2015 led me to speak with a person who contacts spirits. It was a rough period. I had completed my PhD in Old Testament/Hebrew Bible in 2009 but still had not secured a permanent position as a professor. In the intervening years, I had obtained three visiting positions and worked as an adjunct professor. One semester, I taught four classes at three institutions in two states (that did border each other). As is often the case with adjuncts, I was overworked and underpaid. And very tired. Now my third stint in a visiting position was about to end, and I was still without a lasting academic job. My self-doubts rose. Even though I adored teaching as a Bible professor, could I make it in this profession I had entered mid-life?

This particular day I was leading a women's retreat, as I did every spring, for the Presbyterian church where my husband was the senior pastor. I was also feeling hopeful. I had recently completed two sets of multiday interviews as a finalist for positions as a professor at separate theological graduate schools. I thought my lectures and meetings on those campuses had gone well, although

I had felt similarly after previous finalist interviews and received no offer in the end. One of the women attending the church retreat, Alexandra, supported herself as a medium with an office in Manhattan and one in Los Angeles. Wondering if she could offer insights on my job possibilities (read: feeling desperate), I asked Alexandra if she would meet with me to share any clues or cues from the spiritual world.

Alexandra graciously agreed. During a break in the retreat schedule, I went into her very simple lodge bedroom: two twin beds with white sheets and a beige folded blanket at the end of each bed, a mirror, a dresser, and a big window overlooking the woods. She sat on one bed; I sat on the other. Alexandra looked out the window, said the Lord's Prayer, and then waited. After a few moments, the Spirit took over. Alexandra correctly predicted where I would land in a tenure-track position. Then she added, "Write a book . . . in your own voice. . . . Don't wait." But wait I did. In the intervening years, I published scholarly articles and edited two books, but I did not follow these spiritual instructions—until now.

It took me a while to muster the courage to write an academic book that is so personal. Usually scholars try to take themselves out of their research and publications, allowing the evidence to steer the course of discovery and guide the production of knowledge. Of course, no one is ever entirely neutral, and the questions we ask determine the direction the research will take. However, academics rarely incorporate their own hopes and heartaches into their writing. I don't often find my colleagues writing books that divulge information about falling in love with their spouse or their challenges in raising children or huge financial setbacks or tragic deaths in their families, as I do here. I share such personal matters because this book is about the Bible, and the grit, grime, and gains of life are central to biblical stories. Also, as you see how I relate the Bible to my life, I hope you will ponder how it connects to yours.

The close interweaving of personal stories and researched scholarship makes this book unlike any other on feminist interpretation of the Bible that I have read (and I've read lots!). Instead of another book that primarily revisits texts focused on women characters, I seek to offer a fresh contribution to feminist biblical scholarship. Feminism and the Bible both know that there is power in telling our stories. Indeed, that power of honest storytelling is the core of the Bible's impressive ability to stay relevant to our lives.

While incorporating one's life stories is unusual in scholarly books, this approach is inherently biblical. Not only does the Bible share personal stories about the people in its pages, but it also comes from a world where storytelling was vital—and Western academic scholarship was nonexistent. So much of what we read in biblical scholarship comes from traditional (read: male-centered) Eurocentric interpretations, yet this lens is only one of many possible approaches. Still, the post-Enlightenment legacy that privileges rationality is strong. Indeed, modern academics are schooled to spurn claims that are not scientifically proven and backed with lots of evidence. Yet there is irony in bringing only this approach to biblical studies and its ancient world, where our modern concepts of science and rationality are essentially irrelevant. How can we trust the Bible if we do so only based on logic? A sea parts in two so slaves can become free? A dead prophet is brought back to life and lives eternally with God? Those who limit their acceptable concepts to objective reality have no choice but to scoff at such stories. But those with faith or imagination or both still believe in the mysterious truths of the biblical story. As you do when you read the Bible, I invite you to read this book with both head and heart.

. . . . .

Each chapter of *Eve Isn't Evil* explores a different biblical book or section of the Bible, intertwining academic knowledge with stories from my life. I also include stories from people I know: students, relatives, colleagues, and friends. If I am specific about who they are, they have given their permission and are mentioned in the acknowledgments. In some cases, I have obscured key details to protect someone's privacy. All stories are told with honest caring and are devoid of exaggeration, and therefore they are as true as any truth.

I have tried to frame the scholarly conversation in ways that are accessible and hopefully enjoyable to read. This book presumes zero previous knowledge of the Bible. If you are one of those people who knows little about the Bible, know that I was one of them too for almost the first half of my life. Even though I grew up as the daughter of a minister, the biblical passages I heard in church seemed mostly disjointed and often confusing. (In retrospect, it probably would have helped to actually *read* the Bible, but I was busy and had other stuff to do—you know how it goes.) I often felt ignorant and wished I had had a concise Bible "cheat sheet" to provide some simple handles on a very complicated text. If such a guide would be helpful for you, please see appendix 1, Bible Basics, which gives an overview that summarizes every biblical book in one line. In the footnotes of this book, I explain references or terms that might be unfamiliar. Hopefully, these elements will make learning about the Bible less intimidating for you than it often seemed to me.

Of the ten chapters in this book, seven focus explicitly on the Old Testament (or Hebrew Bible), with one chapter on the New Testament, for several reasons. First (and paramount), the Old Testament is my area of expertise. These are the texts that I have studied in depth—and I am eager to share what I have learned. Second, most Christians know significantly more about the New Testament (especially the Gospels, which tell about Jesus' life) than they do about the Old Testament. This leaves Christians with comparatively little knowledge and appreciation of Jesus' Scriptures, which were the Hebrew Scriptures (known to most Christians as the Old Testament). Third, I hope that this book will interest Jewish as well as Christian readers since most of it focuses on Jewish sacred texts. I lament the ways in which Christian interpretation of the Bible has too often been used against Jews. By concentrating primarily on the Hebrew Bible, this book seeks to foster appreciation of Jews and Judaism by exploring texts that are foundational first to Judaism and then to Christianity. Finally, I hope that this book will appeal to any reader who is curious about the Bible. Keeping the focus on the longer of the two testaments familiarizes the reader with more of the Bible's content. One of the reasons the Bible has endured for millennia is its ability to reach our common humanness, regardless of any faith tradition, and to offer uplifting insights about struggle, resilience, and hope.

This introductory chapter, "In the Beginning," is followed by the title chapter, "Eve Isn't Evil." Both introduce key points that are helpful to keep in mind for the rest of the book. The subsequent chapters are arranged in canonical order, loosely corresponding to the progression of related texts in the Hebrew Bible then the New Testament. Parts of my life overlap in these pages: I'll briefly refer to a person or an incident in one chapter and then flesh out a related story more fully in another. The weft of the biblical books and the warp of my own life loosely weave the chapters together.

The subtitle of this book conveys the contents as feminist. I claim "feminist" with a touch of trepidation because this term carries negative connotations for many people. But not for me. To me, feminism simply means liberty and justice for all, including people who identify as female. I do not focus on feminism as a conduit for anger or frustration, although injustices can rightly elicit such responses. Rather, I concentrate on the gifts of feminism, which are self-respect, opportunity, and joy. I recognize my debt to those who fought for rights I have.

For most of human history, women's realms have been confined to domestic spheres. Opportunity for girls and women to go to school have been limited or nonexistent (as it still is in parts of the world). Reaching back just a few generations in my own family history, and perhaps yours too, illustrates these points. My mother came of age in the 1950s and went to secretarial school, not college, as was common for women. Her mother went to school only through eighth grade and then started working as a bookkeeper when she was fourteen. My mother's father was one of fourteen children, only eleven of whom survived to adulthood. My maternal great-grandmother had no access to birth control; my grandfather's family was poor and got poorer with each new baby. My father went to college and graduate school. His mother, who died before I was born, was college educated, which was rare in the early twentieth century, especially for women. She taught Latin and Greek but had to stop as soon as she got married. As a mother and professor who teaches ancient languages myself, I am living a life she could have only imagined. Access to education, birth control, and career possibilities are hard-won gains that are manifest in my life thanks to feminists before me.

While concerns surrounding women's lives are the focus of feminism, anyone who shares its goals can be a feminist. This includes not only men and youth but people of all gender identities. Most of this book operates within the binary sphere of women and men, as does the Bible. There is, however, gender fluidity in the Bible, which I explore in the section "Beyond the Binary" in chapter 10. When possible, I speak of people (not men and women). As recognized in feminist scholarship, I realize that the body is more the receptor than the generator of meaning. Gender identity is a cultural construct, not an intrinsic self that hinges on a body part or genetic blueprint.[1] One can choose to perform gender roles in the ways that society expects or in other ways.

A few more guidelines might be helpful. To speak of the "Old Testament" refers to the first part of the Bible from a Christian perspective. The "Hebrew Bible" is an academic term designating the same books in a different order. I use the terms interchangeably

---

1. For discussion of gender as performance, see Butler, *Gender Trouble*, 8–17.

in this book. In each chapter, I include some discussion of words in their original biblical languages (Hebrew for the Old Testament and Greek for the New Testament).[2] Every translation involves interpretive choices, and no one translation is definitive. I offer alternatives, based on solid scholarship, to open our thinking with different possibilities than those commonly found in printed Bibles. I work from the New Revised Standard Version (abbreviated NRSV), unless otherwise specified. Usually the Hebrew or Greek words are transliterated—that is, written using letters in the English alphabet instead of the Hebrew or Greek characters. Those whose works I cite are Bible scholars, unless otherwise indicated. You can find their scholarship from references in the footnotes, which I have tried, with some success, to keep to a minimum. The essays are followed by questions that invite you to reflect on your own life, in a journal or in conversation with others, perhaps in a Bible study or a book group or a classroom. This book is grounded in the feminist and biblical conviction that honestly sharing stories is empowering. Each chapter also contains a corresponding section in chapter 10 to provide a deeper academic look at an issue raised in the chapter.[3] I also include a brief annotated list of books in appendix 2 called "Resources for Further Exploration" in case you would like to investigate more sources on your own. I write with deep respect for your intelligence as a smart person, because you are.

So I invite you, my new reader friend, to come with me on this creative, academic, personal, feminist exploration of biblical texts. Please bring your open mind. Offering vulnerability, I have taken a risk in writing this book that is different from others in biblical scholarship. Trying a new approach, you take a risk in reading it. But the rewards are many. You will increase your knowledge of

2. Approximately nine chapters of the Bible (passages from Daniel and Ezra) plus a few scattered verses are written in Aramaic, the language that Jesus spoke. However, I do not have a chapter that focuses on these texts.

3. I include Hebrew and Greek in these academic discussions.

the Bible and be introduced to cutting-edge scholarship in a way that is friendly, accessible, and even, at points, humorous. You will discover new aspects of biblical texts and their translations that will surprise and may concern you. You will feel kinship with the Bible's characters as episodes from their lives prompt recollections from yours. You will remember biblical stories better because we recall what we feel, and personal stories are emotionally powerful. You will gain theological insights and become more aware of the Bible's timeless ability to connect with our lives. And—if you are like me—your appreciation of the Bible will be deeper and your faith will be stronger for engaging with biblical texts on multiple meaningful levels.

I hope you will join me as one who loves the Bible as a source of guidance, solace, motivation, companionship, wisdom, and inspiration—but never shame or blame. Feminist interpretation upended my assumptions of the Bible as judgmental, especially regarding women. I was introduced to biblical texts in a way that expanded my mind and my heart, like an interesting, caring friend. That this book might, in some way, do the same for you is my living, writing prayer.

2

Eve Isn't Evil—
Why I Love Her
and You Should Too

Would you kindly go get a pencil or pen, or take out your phone? (I'll wait.) Now, without overthinking, please answer this question: Who are the two most famous women in the Bible?

You can jot down your response below or type it into your phone. Or just say the names aloud.

Were your answers "Eve" and "Mary"? That is my first guess. My second guess, especially if you are a Christian, is that you named "Mary," the mother of Jesus, and "Mary Magdalene," known as a prostitute.

In a show-offy way, I hope I am right. But I would much rather be wrong because these responses say a lot about common understandings of women in the Bible. If women want a well-known biblical role model who matches their gender, the options are sparse. No Moses, David, or Jesus for you—sorry, women! You can either relate to Eve or Mary Magdalene—a fallen sexual seductress or whore (Eve bonus: you ruined the human race!) or to Mary, a virgin mother (good luck with that). These alternatives limit women to the two places where patriarchy wants them: the pedestal (Mary, mother of Jesus) or the pit (Eve/Mary Magdalene).

Oft-repeated biblical interpretations become cultural narratives that run deep. The message that women are left to take not only from the Bible but also from a lot of Western culture boils down to two stark alternatives: (1) you are considered to be beyond mere mortals, like a goddess (a perception mostly foisted on celebrities) and aren't allowed to be real, or (2) you are perceived as unworthy of the same rights, opportunities, income, and respect as men (the rest of us). Belittling ideas about women's worth creep into our psyches and lead to situations that real women deal with every day.

I vividly recall an incident when was I was a young congregational pastor that left me shocked and shaken. One of my responsibilities was to visit and provide pastoral care for people who were homebound. This particular afternoon, I was inside the living room of an elderly man whose wife had recently died. While I cannot remember this man's name, I can picture him clearly. He was in his early seventies with leathery skin and lots of age spots on his face. The top of his head was entirely bald, but two tufts of white hair protruded above each ear, looking as if they held his heavy, rectangular, black-rimmed glasses in place. I (my twenty-something self) would go to his home, sit and listen to him, then take his hands and offer a prayer. On the third visit, after the prayer, he grabbed me and kissed me hard on the mouth. I left and told no one. Not a single friend, not the other pastor of the church, not even my newlywed husband. Why not, I now wonder. Shame? Concern for my reputation and career? A desire to pretend it didn't happen? On some deep level, I think cultural narratives were at play within me. No big deal. Just forget about it—which I obviously have not. Women just put up with abuse.

Our stories either encourage women's acceptance of abuse or challenge it. Our culture is so saturated with a lack of respect for women that we don't even notice its many manifestations. To demonstrate this point, I ask my students a series of questions, with specific instructions just to raise their hands until asked to speak an answer.

Me: "Please raise your hand if you think the English language has a word that means 'hatred of women.'"

Every hand goes up.

Me: "Please keep your hand up if you know what this word is."

Every hand stays up.

Me: "What is that word?"

I call on someone.

A student answers: "Misogyny."

Me: "Correct!"

"Now, please raise your hand if you think the English language has a word that means 'hatred of men.'"

Confused expressions. Students start looking around the room. Are other students raising their hands? A few hands go up, sort of.

Me: "Please keep your hand up if you know what that (possible) word is."

No hands are raised.

Me: "There is a word that means 'hatred of men' in English. That word is 'misandry.' You do not know it because you do not hear it. For the most part, our culture does not use the term 'misandry' or, apparently, need it. But you all knew the word 'misogyny.' What does this tell you?"

We still have a long way to go (understatement).

Biblical stories have been used to devalue women and limit their options because of *what we are told they mean*. Surprisingly, though, a lot of what we think is in the Bible comes from interpreters' biases and not the text itself.

The story of Eve offers an insightful example. This myth is about three thousand years old, and interpretations of Eve as evil are about two thousand years old.[1] Women have been denied dignity and power in various economic, cultural, and religious forms because of what we have been taught about Eve. For an extreme example of how the Bible has been used to vilify women, consider the witch trials, which primarily took place from the fifteenth to seventeenth centuries. During these trials, tens of thousands to hundreds of thousands of women were tortured and executed as witches who supposedly inherited their wickedness from Eve.[2] Many people think of Eve as a sinful, selfish seductress. Yet so many of our presumptions about the first woman are not in the Bible. (Details, details.)

But the good news is that we can retell Bible stories in new ways. We can reinterpret biblical narratives to build women up or at least not tear them down. Instead of seeing Eve as the trashy temptress who introduces original sin into the world, we can understand her as the pinnacle of creation. That telling of Genesis 1–3 might go like this:

God Creates the World: Take 1 (Gen. 1–2:4a)

Long ago and far away, the world met a God who was wondrous. She had the amazing ability to do with her words what women do with their bodies: create life. On Day 1, God decided it was time. Time to

1. A myth is a story with supernatural characters set in an ancient past; myths reveal timeless truths.

2. The book *Malleus Maleficarum* (or "Hammer of Witches"), written by Heinrich Kramer and Jacob Springer and published in 1486 by Peter Drach in Speyer, Germany, was one of the first books widely distributed through the invention of the printing press. This immensely popular work had tremendous influence in promoting the execution of women. Part 1, Question 6 explains that "in the Old Testament the Scriptures have much that is evil to say about women, and this because of the first temptress, Eve, and her imitators" (https://www.sacred-texts.com/pag/mm/index .htm). William Phipps documents the history of women as descendants of Eve being oppressed for millennia, as well as persecuted, tortured, and even killed. See Phipps, *Genesis and Gender*, 55–66 (esp. 61–62).

explode into the world by forming it. She knew about chaos because those swirlings were of her—but now there would be light—like the shining energy a baby sees when she pops forth from her mother's birth canal. The messy waters burst suddenly—and there is light and life! So God created light, leading to life. She then took a week of her godly life and made all of creation: day and night; the heavens; seas, dry land, and plants; sun and moon; birds and fish; land animals; and finally (in God's own image!) people (Gen. 1:1–2:1). At the end of all that work, God paid attention to self-care and took a day of rest—the most special day of all—and the world was complete (2:2–4a).[3] Like many of us after a big project, God was tired, but she was also pleased. Because God saw that her creation was good—even very good.[4]

Perhaps the most noticeable liberty in my retelling of this creation story is the gender of God. Pronouns for God are a real sticky wicket for us feminists who love the Bible. The Hebrew of the Old Testament and the Greek of the New Testament are gendered languages. The pronouns and verbs referring to God are masculine. Yet language gendered as masculine does not mean that the subject of that word is male. For example, in Hebrew the word for bird (*of*) is masculine and the word for large animals (*behemah*) is feminine. Obviously, not all birds are male and not all large animals are female. The grammatical gender is not the same as the biological or claimed gender.

Most people I know do not think that God has a gender. They believe that God is constrained by nothing, including our constructs that label people as male, female, nonbinary, transgender,

3. The small "a" indicates the first part of the verse; "b" indicates the second part. The first creation story ends in the middle of a verse.

4. The theory of evolution gives a scientific explanation for creation; the Bible gives a sacred explanation. One is not wrong and the other right—the two understandings are just different. I remind those in my classes that they too are creations. I know each person as a learner, whereas their parents know the same individual as the child they have raised. Am I right to think, "He's my student!" and the parents wrong to think, "He's my son!"? Of course not. Both are correct. We just understand the same (human) creation differently.

or another sexual identity. Yet those same people feel perfectly comfortable referring to God as male because this language is traditional, convenient, familiar, and biblical. And as some Christians say, "If it's good enough for Jesus, it's good enough for me."

When we talk about language, we are really talking about power. Speaking of God only in masculine terms is not good enough for me because of all the ruinous ramifications of deifying maleness. Jesus refers to God as male because his culture could not have accepted any alternatives. Ours can—or we can at least try. I wish I could read and teach the Bible in Korean or Chinese, where the personal pronoun for "he" or "she" is the same. But unfortunately, I do not know these languages, so I refer to God with a combination of "he," "she," and "they." To confine God to male pronouns limits God. And that is a theological phallacy (*sic*).

Back to our creation story. After Genesis 1:1–2:4a, which tells of the world being made and put in order, we get another version of creation that begins with nothing once again.[5] This story starts with the first person, who is neither male nor female but an earth creature made from the ground.[6]

God Creates the World: Take 2 (Gen. 2:4b–3:24)

There was nothing on the earth because there was no one to take care of it (Gen. 2:4b–5). God first made sure there was plenty of

---

5. The juxtaposition of two creation stories in Genesis is evidenced by multiple factors, including contradictions between the two texts. Genesis 1:12 describes God's creation of plants, and in 1:29 God gives those plants to people for food. Conversely, 2:5 portrays a world "when no plant of the field was yet in the earth and no herb of the field had yet sprung up" at the start of the second creation story.

6. The word for "earth creature" in Hebrew is *adam*, and the word for "earth" is *adamah*. Translators decide for readers if *adam* means "human," "man," or "Adam." In my continued retelling of the creation story below, I translate the Hebrew word *adam* in all three of these ways, depending on where it appears in the story. When it refers to the initial human, I translate *adam* as "human" or "person." Once the woman is created, I translate *adam* as "man." After the woman is named Eve, I translate *adam* as Adam.

water, which is necessary for life (v. 6). Then God took some earth and molded it into the first living being and filled it with the breath of life (v. 7). Next God put all kinds of plants in the garden, including the tree of the knowledge of good and evil and the tree of life. Just to be sure this garden was paradise, God added lots of rivers (getting fresh water was hard work in the ancient world) and quality metals and precious jewels (to throw in some sparkle). God then placed the human in the garden to take care of it (vv. 8–15). The human could eat of any plant, with one exception: the tree of the knowledge of good and evil. Violation penalty: death (vv. 16–17). God realized that this human should not be alone, so God created animals. These creatures then paraded before the human, who named them (vv. 18–20).

I imagine this scene like a zoological beauty pageant. Strutting as tall and proud as they can in their wild assortment of colors, sizes, and shapes, the animals file by the human, who points and provides designations like "rhinoceros," "aardvark," "orangutan," (and naturally) "bird of paradise." Then later, as the human gets less creative from decision fatigue: "bat," "cat," "gnat," "rat"— just live with it! As in any competition, there is suspense. Who will get to partner with the human? Chameleon? Wouldn't work. Giraffe? Doubt it. Cockroach? No way! Chimpanzee?? Closer . . . but the human needs a true partner (the Hebrew words here are *ezer kenegdo*; Gen. 2:20), and none of these animals will do.

Most English Bibles say that God creates the *ezer* as a "helper."[7] This translation implies that the next creature is the assistant or subordinate, the one who will get the coffee and tidy up after the important people have left the cosmic room. But the phrase *kenegdo* conveys one on par as an equal.[8] And most of the time

---

7. For example, the ESV, NASB, NJB, NJPS, and NRSV translations render *ezer* as "helper;" the KJV translates it as "help meet."

8. The phrase *kenegdo* is from the preposition *neged* meaning "that which corresponds to," "in front of," and "before." Koehler, Baumgartner, and Stamm, *Hebrew and Aramaic Lexicon*, 666.

the word *ezer* appears in the Bible, it refers to *God*.[9] For this final creature to be made as an *ezer* is to be likened to the Divine, at least in biblical understanding.

Since none of the animals was perfectly suited for the human, God considerately first put the person in a deep sleep under godly anesthesia. God then took one of the bones from the side of this creature—not from the head (to rule above) or from the feet (to be below) but from the rib (to accompany alongside)—then attentively stitched up the wound. And voilà! God created a woman! This *ezer*-human was the crowning of creation, just as the final special day of rest had been the pinnacle of God's first formation of the world. Now there were two sexually differentiated creatures: the man and the woman (Gen. 2:21–23). The man radically proclaimed their stunning equality because they were *of the same substance*: "Bone of my bones and flesh of my flesh!" (v. 23a). To be sure that the man knew his place as the penultimate human, the man must leave his father and mother to cling to the woman, signaling her power and strength, as well as his need of her. Like the babes of humanity that they were, the man and woman were naked but did not care (vv. 24–25).

It was paradise.

Enter the smart snake.[10] The snake approached the decision-maker of the couple (the woman) and asked about the "do not eat" prohibition: "Did God say, 'You [plural] shall not eat from any tree in the garden?'" (Gen. 3:1). The woman explained that they could eat from any tree in the garden, but they must not eat—or even touch—the tree in the middle of the garden, or else they will die (vv. 2–3). How did she even know this? The woman had not yet been

9. See, for example, Exod. 18:4; Deut. 33:7; and Pss. 70:6; 121:1; 146:5. Those familiar with the work of Old Testament scholar Dr. Phyllis Trible will recognize my indebtedness to my former professor on this point and throughout this retelling. Her revolutionary exegesis of Gen. 2–3 opened my eyes (see 3:7) to the strength of Eve as our biblical foremother. See her chapter "A Love Story Gone Awry" in Trible, *God and the Rhetoric of Sexuality*, 72–143.

10. For an engaging account of Eve and Adam's story from the snake's perspective, see Archer, "Not Sneaky but Smart."

formed when God told the earth creature to avoid the tree of good and evil (2:16–17). Maybe this knowledge came with the substance of humanness. The snake assured the woman that the couple would not die (3:4). Rather, they would gain the divine ability to know the difference between good and evil (v. 5).[11]

The woman was bright. She had the divine *ezer* spark, and like most people, she got smart by following her curiosity. Now she had the chance to know good from evil and to learn about ethics; this was exciting. Still, wanting to make her way carefully and judiciously in the world, the woman gave the matter serious thought. She saw that the tree was good for food, delighted the senses, and, most compellingly, was desired to make her wise. After contemplation, she took a piece of this intelligence-giving fruit and ate it. Further, being the generous and considerate person that she was, the woman shared this food with her partner (Gen. 3:6).

The man had been with the woman throughout this interchange, just listening silently, as he generally did around her, seeking to learn what he could. Here she was trying to teach him about conversational skills and decision-making. Had he been more of a helper himself, he might have spoken up and reminded the woman of God's instructions, instead of remaining quiet. But he said nothing because, again, he was not wearing the pants in the relationship—although no one was wearing clothes yet. However, the man did happen to be hungry, so he ate the fruit without a moment's hesitation, much less a word of protest—or thanks, for that matter. With his fateful bite, people would come to learn that there is both bad and good in the world and that disobeying God has consequences. Yet the serpent was right because the man and woman did not die that day, as God had specified (Gen. 2:16–17). [No death of either Adam or Eve is reported until Adam was nearly a thousand years old (5:5), which is not a bad run.][12]

---

11. The Hebrew in v. 5 specifies that the woman and man would become like gods (with a plural noun and verb), not God, as most English Bibles read.

12. Genesis 5:5 gives Adam's age at death as 930 years old. The long life spans of people in the first chapters of Genesis underscore the mythological nature of these texts.

Also, as the serpent predicted, the couple knew more than they had before (Gen. 3:4-5). First, they realized that they were naked. Luckily for them, amid the knowledge they had acquired in eating the fruit must have been the ability to make clothing out of fig leaves (or the closest to clothing that you can make out of fig leaves, which fortunately are fairly large), and they stitched together some leaf-clothes (3:7).

At this point, God was on her evening garden stroll. The man and woman heard her getting closer. They knew that they had done something wrong and got out of sight—fast—crouching behind garden trees (Gen. 3:8). God called out for the man (v. 9). Perhaps realizing the futility of trying to hide from God (in her own garden, no less), the man spoke up: "I heard the sound of you in the garden, and I was afraid, because I was naked; and I hid myself" (v. 10). Focusing on himself, he made no mention of the woman who was there with him. It dawned on God that something was wrong, and she asked, "Who told you that you were naked?" (v. 11). God wondered how the man even *knew* about nakedness. God then asked the man if *he* ate of the fruit of the tree of knowledge of good and evil after she specifically told *him* not to do so (2:17; 3:11). He had been caught.

Yet the man, sadly, was not self-aware. Instead of directly owning his mistake, he took the route well-worn by cowards and diverted the blame elsewhere. First, he threw his partner under the proverbial bus, and then he dared to insult God. "The *woman* whom *you* gave to be with me, *she* gave me fruit from the tree." Then he mumbled, quickly as an afterthought because the evidence could not be denied, "And I ate" (Gen. 3:12). God, in her grace, let the man's self-centeredness slide.

God then asked the woman directly what she had done. Unlike the man, the woman did not cast blame on her partner, who clearly had heard God's prohibition but showed no reluctance in eating the fruit. And the woman wouldn't dream of accusing the Deity herself. Instead, the woman rightfully informed God that eating of the fruit was the snake's suggestion and then admitted to her own culpability (Gen. 3:13). God did not ask the serpent any questions directly, because the divine spark *ezer*-woman was so trustworthy that she could always be believed.

Then God did what every responsible parent does—she revealed the consequences of the actions taken by the man, woman, and snake. The serpent would now have to crawl on the ground—eat dust, snake!—and people would hate snakes, which lots of people do (Gen. 3:14–15). The woman would now have to go through labor (Hebrew: *itsavon*) when giving birth.[13] Plus, she, as the ultimate human being, must look charitably upon the man and allow him to have some role in ruling the created order (v. 16). The man was punished for putting the woman above God and for ignoring the prohibition about eating from the tree. This male human was in the habit of heeding and following the female, but choosing her over God had crossed a line. Since the man did not respect the commandment specifically given to the human (*adam*), the earth (*adamah*) of his own substance was cursed to work against him (v. 17). Instead of lush plants, his labor (Hebrew: *itsavon*) would yield thorns and thistles (v. 18). He was condemned to eat the plants and his food in the sweat (snot?) of his nose (v. 19a).[14] The punishments and the way God spoke to the couple revealed that the woman was God's favorite. The work of childbirth is temporary. The man's punishment of toiling for food day in, day out, year in, and year out is constant, as is the snake's slithering on the ground. In a final reminder to be humble, God informed the man that his ultimate destiny will be the earth from which he was taken. He is dust, and to dust he must return (v. 19b).

The man became appropriately contrite. His very name, Adam, reveals his connection with the lowly and now cursed ground (*adamah*; Gen. 3:17). The hated serpent eats dust (v. 14); the man's ultimate destiny is to become serpent food (v. 19). But the woman, like God, can create life. Even her punishment highlights her amazing

---

13. The Hebrew word *itsavon* is usually translated as "pain" but more accurately means "toil" or "labor." See the section "Misleading Translations of Genesis 3:6 and 3:16" on p. 132 in chapter 10 of this book.

14. The Hebrew in Gen. 3:19 describes *zeat appekha*, which means "sweat of your nostrils" (not "sweat of your face," as we read in English).

ability, while keeping her mortal through the work of birthing children. In his epiphany of recognizing her superiority, the man proclaimed her name as Eve (Hebrew for "life-giver"). She is the mother of all living creatures, like the God who created her (v. 20). This stunningly laudatory recognition was Adam's roundabout way of apologizing for not intervening before the woman took fruit from the tree and for later diverting all the blame away from himself.

God looked approvingly on Adam's attempt at reconciliation. Showing sartorial mercy to the couple, the Divine Designer made them fur coats (Gen. 3:21). But even God was a little nervous. She trusted Eve but was worried about Adam. He might go ahead and eat from the tree of life, trying to be like God (v. 22). He had heard the prohibition (2:16–17) and promptly ignored it, and then he tried blaming Eve for the disobedience (3:12), even though he too had eaten the fruit (v. 6). What if he took from the tree that would make him live forever, like God (v. 22)? The risk was too great. God then sent him out of the garden, east of Eden (v. 23). His spirit ground down, he will bend down and work the ground. But still suspecting that the boy-man could not be trusted, God put an angel with a flaming sword to guard the tree of life (v. 24). Only God will be immortal.

And Eve? She remained in Eden with God—the mother of all living with the Mother of Creation. Whenever you see a mother and daughter laughing together, that is a spark of God and Eve. Whenever you notice two women sharing stories and supporting each other, that is a trace of the divine mother-daughter. Wherever two or three women or girls are gathered in her name, God is there among them. Eventually, Eve realized the need to share her life-giving power with the rest of the world, so she generously left the garden and joined Adam to have children (Gen. 4:1–2). And Eve (the life-giver) and God (the Creator) continue to birth humanity, savoring their wondrous ability to form life, rejoicing in their wise and glorious creation.

• • • • •

Is this the story of Adam and Eve the way it has been told to you? Let me go out on a limb and guess that it is not. If you identify as male, you might even find this telling of Eve and Adam's story hard to read.

How does it feel?

Regardless of your gender identity, you likely found a few elements of this story surprising, but the Hebrew text undergirds the interpretation above. Did you know that only the first human (*adam*) was told not to eat of the fruit of the tree of knowledge? The woman was not even created yet when God gave this fateful prohibition (Gen. 2:16–17; 2:22). When the serpent talks to the woman, the man is present throughout the entire conversation (3:6). In Hebrew, it is clear that the snake addresses both the man and the woman because he uses plural pronouns (this is obscured in English since "you" is both singular and plural), which is why the woman answers with "we," not "I" (vv. 1–2). Genesis 3:6 specifically says that the man is "with her" (Hebrew: *immah*), but many English translations of the Bible leave out the word *immah*, creating the impression that the man is not present.[15] At the end of the story in Genesis 3:23–24, the *adam* is made to leave the garden. The Hebrew of 3:23 specifies that God sent him (not "them") out of Eden. The next verse reiterates that only the man (*ha-adam*) is driven out and kept from reentering the garden (v. 24). Perhaps Eve stays with God.

So why does the woman get all the blame for the "fall"—a word nowhere in the text—of humanity? A feminist scholar once told me, in so many words, "I have no need of the Bible—you can have it," even though she was a Christian theologian. She particularly hated the story of Eve because of what she had been told about Eve's supposed deviousness, imparted to all women. But Eve is not the ancient foremother who dooms every person to a life of

---

15. This issue is also discussed in "Misleading Translations of Genesis 3:6 and 3:16" on p. 132 in chapter 10 of this book.

sin and disobedience. She is a pioneering theologian who wrestles with the words of God. She is a thoughtful decision-maker who thinks before she acts. She is a curious seeker of knowledge who yearns to understand ethics so she can make her way in the world. She is the mythical mother of all discerning people. I am proud to be a child of the mother of all living—and I hope you are too.

Whether the Bible is beloved or reviled, its power is in the interpretation. Know that there is no one "right" way to interpret the Bible. There are just acceptable ways—interpretations that a given community will tolerate or embrace, then adopt, use, and share. But there are wrong and unacceptable ways to interpret the Bible—and those are ways that are harmful to someone, including yourself. Regrettably, such weaponizing interpretations are all too common. Yet instead of rejecting the Bible or ignoring it or finding it too overwhelming, we can explore the meanings and the mysteries of its textual terrain. Like Eve, we can question and engage what we come to discover through the word of God.

Eve and Adam are our mythological ancestors who reveal timeless truths. Like them, we are faced with choices that have consequences. We work hard; we contribute to the continuation of life; we discover a world that is beautiful, terrible, and full of wonder. With awe, we carry this awareness as we make our way through our days—and this reverence for the creation we are is good, even very good.

──────── **Questions for Reflection and Conversation** ────────

1. Our culture commonly understands Eve as evil, but a close look at the text reveals her many positive qualities, including a desire for wisdom, along with openness, honesty, curiosity, discernment, and generosity. What qualities of Eve live on in you? How and when do you show or share these traits?

2. Biblical interpretation has frequently maligned Eve and, by association, all women. How do you think your life would be different if you had another gender identity?

3. Eve is given the amazing ability to nurture life in her own body, and she is called "the mother of all living." What do you like to create? If you could be called the "mother/father/parent" of something, what would it be?

Think Your
Family's a Mess?
Biblical Families R Us

I f only I had been paying closer attention to stories of families in Genesis, perhaps I would not have been so devastated when I received the autism diagnosis for my son. I would have seen that some people are viewed as "other" through no fault of their own. I would have known that children are their own people in ways their parents never anticipate. I would have noticed biblical fathers and mothers whose offspring have abilities they cannot comprehend. But despite the scriptural nuggets offering meaty insights, my maternal mind craved the feel-good emotional equivalent of cream puffs. I grew up on a steady diet of family-friendly sitcoms (looking at you, *Brady Bunch*), where families were cheerful and well-groomed, and all issues were tidily resolved in a half hour. Genesis, like life, teaches otherwise.

When I ask my students what "genesis" means, they invariably tell me "beginning." True, but the Greek word *genesis* is also translated as "origin." (The stem of *genesis* relates to many English words, like *gene*, *gene*alogy, and [yes] *geni*tals—where we *origin*ate!)[1] Genesis explains the origins of the world in chapters 1–11, which scholars call the primeval history, and the origins of Israel's people in chapters 12–50, as understood by its ancient writers. Genesis 12–50 is often dubbed the stories of the patriarchs (Abraham, Isaac, and Jacob). However, without the matriarchs (Sarah, Rebekah, Leah, and Rachel), no one is getting beyond one *gene*ration, so we more accurately refer to Genesis 12–50 as the stories of the ancestors.

Israel's family begins with one man: Abraham (originally named Abram), who would today be considered an Iraqi immigrant. This "exalted father," which is what "Abram" means in Hebrew, comes from Ur (Gen. 11:31). A city on the Euphrates River in the realm of Sumer (modern-day Iraq), Ur was located not far from the Persian Gulf. Abraham's story is set in the late Bronze Age, a little less than two thousand years before the year zero. At this time, Ur had writing (big invention!), job specialization (astounding innovation!), and centers of civilization with communal buildings (amazing! cities!). Trade, writing, art, and architecture thrived well over a thousand years before they emerged in the unknown land where God sends Abraham (12:1). Why would you willingly forsake the Paris of your day (Ur) for Nowheresville (Canaan)? But God calls Abraham, who walks where God tells him to go, physically answering the ultimate theological question: Where are your feet? What do you do, where do you go, as a result of what you profess? Talking about your belief in God (or anything else) is a lot easier than walking into an unknown that God sets before you.

When Abraham leaves home, his world changes. He trusts and obeys the directive of a mystery god who instructs him to start a

---

1. The words "gene" and "genealogy" descend directly from Greek roots, whereas "genital" is from a similar Latin word meaning "to beget." Both Greek and Latin are part of the same Indo-European language family.

new people. But as much as he yearns to live into God's promise, even a man with an auspicious name like "exalted father" cannot produce a baby without a woman's awesome Eve-like power to nurture and birth life. Abraham has his wife, Sarah.

With God as their advocate, you might expect all to go smoothly for Abraham and Sarah, but strife is baked into life. After ten years living in Canaan and still no baby, they try to have a child in a way that seems like the prerogative of a modern, Western, rich couple but was widespread in antiquity: they take a surrogate (Gen. 16:1–3). Sarah has a slave from the northeastern corner of Africa—the young Egyptian Hagar—whom she gives to old Mesopotamian Abraham for sex (v. 4). Hagar conceives and bears Ishmael, Abraham's firstborn son (v. 15). The first child in the ancestor stories descends from two people who today would be seen as an African woman and an Iraqi man. In Ishmael, whose name means "God hears," worlds come together.

I was recently struck by the relevance of Hagar and Sarah's story when talking with a friend of mine named Alice. Alice is a member of the Bamessing ethnic group in Cameroon, a French- and English-speaking nation on the west coast of central Africa. She was born into a large polygamous family in which children were plentiful (seventeen of them!) but food not so much. Through a series of well-aligned opportunities, Alice managed to combine education with lots of hard work, eventually becoming a Bible professor. From her I have learned how the story of Sarah and Hagar continues to unfold from antiquity to today. Among the Bamessing people, women who are infertile often experience trauma due to the expectations of their culture. Rich women who are unable to conceive instruct their husbands to marry poor women who can have children. The wealthy but barren wife then claims the surrogate's child as her own. Both women are trapped. Unless the infertile first wife can claim to have a child for her husband, she is considered worthless and receives no inheritance. Unless the fertile but poor wife bears a child with the man—who may resort to rape to impregnate her—she will starve. Alice underscores that the women are not to blame for this abuse. Rather, their patriarchal culture gives them no choice if they want to stay alive.[2]

Perhaps like the rich but infertile women of the Bamessing ethnic group, Sarah gets the baby she wants—but she does not embrace Hagar's son as her own. Abraham names and circumcises Ishmael (Gen. 16:15; 17:23), and Hagar, the slave girl from Africa, becomes the mother of Abraham's firstborn son.[3] Abraham eventually has three wives: Sarah, Hagar, and the often overlooked Keturah (25:1–4). But it is African Hagar and Ishmael of mixed heritage who generate the first lineage in the ancestor stories.[4]

The key role of Hagar may surprise you or even feel unsettling; Sarah seems unsettled too. In an unheralded act of feminist support, God responds to Sarah's unabated desire for a child, even after Ishmael is born. Messengers arrive at Sarah and Abraham's home and promise that postmenopausal Sarah will bear a son herself (Gen. 18:10). Sarah laughs—in wonder? delight? disbelief?—but indeed conceives and gives birth to Isaac (21:1–5). His lineage becomes the people of Israel who are eventually called Jews. Ishmael's ancestors become the people of Mohammed who are eventually called Muslims. (The Bible tells the Jewish story and the Quran tells the Islamic story.[5]) Sarah's miraculous motherhood,

2. For further discussion, see Yafeh-Deigh, "Children, Motherhood."

3. Both integral to and outcast in the biblical story, Hagar is a pioneer. The first mother in the ancestor stories is also the first person in the ancestor stories to be visited by an angel, the only woman promised a multitude of offspring, and the only person in the Bible to name God (Gen. 16:7–13). For foundational discussions, see Trible, *Texts of Terror*, 9–36; and Weems, *Just a Sister Away*, 1–21.

4. Foreshadowing both Moses, who leads twelve Israelite tribes, and Jesus, who has twelve disciples, Ishmael is the father of twelve princes (Gen. 17:20; 25:16). He is also a biblical pioneer—like mother, like son. For discussion of similarities among Ishmael, Moses, and Jesus as children, see Parker, "Call Them Ishmael."

5. Abraham and Hagar's son, Ishmael, is mentioned seventeen times in the Bible. (Other characters in the Bible are named Ishmael, but these characters do not refer to the same person.) In the Quran, Ishmael is mentioned twelve times and has a prominent role in Islamic tradition (Quran 2:125, 127, 133, 136, 140; 3:84; 4:163; 6:86; 14:39; 19:54; 21:85; 38:48). For further discussion, see deClaissé-Walford, "Ishmael."

while joyful and uplifting, can also be painful and depressing for women who want children but are unable to conceive.

What comfort might the Bible offer to a woman or a couple with strong faith, like Abraham and Sarah, who hope to have a baby but cannot? Sometimes the Bible is used cruelly. A person may suggest, "If you had faith like Abraham and Sarah, God would give you children too." Telling someone this feels mean—heaping blame and shame on top of heartache. Yet the Bible might still offer creative solace to couples who suffer when their hopes of having a child are dashed, month after devastatingly disappointing month. Genesis resolutely portrays families that form in all kinds of ways and that take varied configurations, usually having endured many hardships along the way.[6] The Bible is also generous with angels or messengers who say, in essence, "God has not forgotten you" (see Gen. 16:5–14). The same Hebrew word, *malakh*, means both "messenger" and "angel"; translators decide whether readers envision a human messenger or a heavenly one. Once we start noticing earthly envoys bringing hints of the divine to our lives, we might be surprised how frequently they appear. Those who are God-sent lead us toward comfort and joy.

Sarah and Abraham heed their messengers and have their long-awaited child, Isaac (Gen. 21:1–8). In one of the most famous scenes in Genesis, Abraham takes his fiercely desired, Sarah-borne son and brings him to the top of a mountain to kill him as sacrifice, as commanded by God. In the nick of time, an angel intervenes and the boy is spared (22:1–14). But look closely at the rest of Isaac's story. He never talks with his father again. In the next chapter of Genesis, Sarah dies (23:1–2). Perhaps the trauma of what her husband had attempted was just too much to bear. Even when the outcome of a situation seems okay, the consequences

---

6. For discussion of the difficulties families face in Genesis and their connection to modern life, see Helsel and Park, *Flawed Family*. Three chapters relate to stories about Abraham, Sarah, and Hagar, focusing on family moves (pp. 47–58), infertility (pp. 59–71), and blended families (pp. 73–86).

of what happened in our family can still affect us, sometimes in devastating ways.

Abraham is left to provide a bride for Isaac, so the father dispatches his trusted servant to the region from which he has come (Gen. 24:1–10). Reflecting this practice of obtaining a wife from one's own land, both my great-grandfather and my husband's grandfather married a woman from "the old country." My husband's grandmother was born and raised in Volos, Greece, and my great-grandmother came from a small village outside Utrecht in Holland. When the men from their hometowns who had immigrated to the United States needed wives, relatives brought these young women across the Atlantic. As each bride-to-be separately stepped in her finest, yet worn, button-up leather shoes onto the gangplanks of the boats that would carry her to a new life, she barely knew the former neighbor who would become her husband. Once married, both women became "take charge" (read: not so warm) matriarchs. But how hard must it have been for them to be uprooted from their homes and thrust into an alien land with a foreign language, never to see their family of origin again?

Abraham's servant is on a similar mission: get a wife from the old country and bring her to marry Isaac, whom she has never met. The servant prays that when he arrives God will send a young woman to draw water for him and his camels. Just as in a Dickens novel, a remarkable coincidence transpires right on time. No sooner does the servant finish speaking than Rebekah emerges at the well. (Wells were the watering holes where marriageable young people met around a desirable drink, like bars today.) You only get one chance to make a first impression, and Rebekah makes a good one. Not only does she offer Abraham's servant water, but she gets water for his ten (!) camels (Gen. 24:10–20). A camel can easily drink thirty gallons of water in a few minutes. Hardworking, hospitable Rebekah must fetch around three hundred gallons of water in a heavy pottery jar! She meets the moment filled with dramatic potential and wildly surpasses expectations.

The servant quickly concludes that this industrious woman is the answer to his prayer (vv. 21, 26).

The text also offers a nod to women's often overlooked labor. In the biblical world (as in many areas of the world today), hauling water was (and is) the task of women and girls.[7] This chore is one example of the unacknowledged, unappreciated, make-the-world-turn everyday work of women. Women still do lots of invisible labor, including unpaid childcare, cleaning, elder care, and cooking. At least Rebekah's efforts are noticed.

Abraham's servant moves quickly to "put a ring on it," and Rebekah receives a nose ring. She invites the servant and his entourage to her home. Abraham's servant recounts his mission to Rebekah's family and then showers them with gifts, and the marriage deal is sealed (Gen. 24:22–53). Amazingly, though, Rebekah is not just shipped off to a new land. Her mother and brother want her to stay with them a little longer, perhaps realizing that they will never see her again. Rebekah's family members directly ask her if she wants to marry Isaac. Her consent matters (vv. 54–59).

Once Rebekah, like Abraham, agrees to venture forth to an unknown land, she is also blessed with a promise of progeny.

Rebekah's blessing (Gen. 24:60)	Abraham's blessing (Gen. 22:17)
"May you, our sister, become thousands of myriads;	"I will indeed bless you and I will make your offspring as numerous as the stars of heaven and as the sand that is on the seashore.
may your offspring gain possession of the gates of their foes."	And your offspring shall possess the gate of their enemies."

Interestingly, the text connects Abraham's blessing to Rebekah. In this couple, she is the power player. The Bible refers to Rebekah's

7. Drawing water was women's work. Marsman, *Women in Ugarit and Israel*, 724.

home as "her mother's household" (Gen. 24:28). The phrase "father's household," appears over 130 times in the Bible; the phrase "mother's household" appears just four times, in stories that highlight women's power (see also Ruth 1:8; Song 3:4; 8:2). Carol Meyers suggests that Rebekah's story may have had its origins in women's storytelling.[8] Perhaps women even wrote Rebekah's story.

People commonly assume that only men wrote the Bible. Ask someone how they know that no woman ever had a hand in producing biblical texts and the argument breaks down quickly.

"Well," they might say, "men were the ones who knew how to write."

"But we have evidence of women's writing in the ancient Near East," you respond, knowledgeable person that you are.

You even bring up an example. "The first known writer in antiquity was Enheduanna, daughter of King Sargon of Akkad. She was a priest and poet at Ur in Sumer, Abraham's place of origin. You can Google her."

Your conversation partner stammers.

We just don't know exactly who nearly all the Bible writers were.

When academics reach a definitive conclusion without definitive evidence, there is an erudite term for this deductive procedure. We call it "bad scholarship." The Bible was written by men, but maybe not entirely. We refer to the writers of certain books as "Malachi" or "Habakkuk," but we have no way of knowing if an actual person by these names wrote these books. How could we? Only if we had outside sources contemporary with biblical texts backing these claims of authorship. And we don't. So when we have documentation of women writing in the Bible and in the ancient world more widely[9] (usually from the upper echelons of

8. Meyers, "Rebekah," 144.
9. Literacy was rare in the ancient Near East, but the Bible still testifies to elite women's ability to write. Two queens, Jezebel of Israel and Esther of Persia, write

society, like Enheduanna), and we know that the Bible is written by a collection of unknown writers, and some of the Bible's stories are dominated by women (like the story of Rebekah and Isaac), and many hands contributed to the formation of these texts over long periods of time, why are we so confident that no woman ever had anything to do with writing parts of the Bible?

Perhaps as further evidence of ancient women's involvement in biblical stories, the ancestor narratives hinge on the women.[10] Abraham's child by Sarah, not Hagar or Keturah, becomes the Bible's focus. The blessing of progeny, first given to Abraham, is connected to Rebekah. After trying unsuccessfully to conceive, Rebekah and Isaac eventually have twins: the instant-older Esau (the firstborn) and then Jacob (Gen. 25:21–26). The sons are very different. Esau is an outdoor hunter, and Jacob is an indoor tent dweller (v. 27). In an outright show of parental favoritism, the father prefers Esau and the mother, Jacob (v. 28). The son with the maternal advocate fares far better.

Through clever and deceptive maneuvering (Gen. 27), Jacob continues the promise given first to Abraham and then to Rebekah (28:3–4). But of course he cannot produce a family without a woman willing to join with him and share her Eve-like power to nurture and birth life. Jacob goes back to Rebekah's homeland (v. 5), and he encounters his future bride by a well (29:1–13). Sound familiar?

You only get one chance to make a first impression, and Jacob makes a good one.

Upon arriving near his mother's people, Jacob sees shepherds with their flocks gathered around a well with a large stone over

---

documents themselves that convey royal authority (see 1 Kings 21:8–9; Esther 9:29). For information on women writing in the ancient Near East, see Lion, "Literacy and Gender"; Marsman, *Women in Ugarit and Israel*, 409–11, 428–29, 688; Snell, *Life in the Ancient Near East*, 53; and Stol, *Women in the Ancient Near East*, 367–71.

10. For further discussion, see "The Status of Women in the Biblical World" on p. 135 in chapter 10 of this book.

it. Since the stone covering the well's opening is so heavy, the first shepherds to arrive must wait for more herders so they can move the stone together and share the water. Newcomer Jacob asks these shepherds if they know his uncle Laban. At just that moment, in another remarkable Dickensian coincidence, Rachel, Laban's daughter, comes to the well. She is a shepherd (girls were shepherds too).[11] Beholding this skilled, hard-working, beautiful young woman approaching with her healthy hordes of shuffling sheep, Jacob is smitten. He falls in love with the whole package. Rachel is attractive, industrious, rich, and has all the right family connections. In a burst of testosterone-charged strength, Jacob hauls away the heavy stone over the well's mouth (which normally requires the combined muscle of many shepherds) and waters Rachel's flock. Like his mother who drew water for ten camels, Jacob meets the moment filled with dramatic potential and wildly surpasses expectations.

Life gave a person I was dating an opportunity-charged moment too. We were in the stomach-fluttering, goo-goo eyed, euphoric phase of a budding love. After seeing a Broadway matinee (*Sarafina!*), we were strolling uptown near Lincoln Center in the early evening, flirting while holding hands. Just as we were crossing West Sixty-First Street, my date suddenly dropped my hand and dashed into the line of moving cars. An older man with disheveled, greasy clothes and a grisly gray beard was lying in the street. A car, whose driver apparently did not see the man, was heading toward him. In a flash, my date positioned his body between the man in the street and the oncoming vehicle, throwing his hands up in the air. "Stop! STOP!!" he yelled at the car—just in time to save the person's life. The man on the asphalt got up and (rather casually,

---

11. Genesis 29:9 specifically says that Rachel is a *roah*, the Hebrew word for "shepherd" in the feminine form. Translators sometimes take away Rachel's occupation. For example, the NRSV translates Gen. 29:9b as follows: "Rachel came with her father's sheep; for she kept them." A more accurate translation reads, "Rachel came with her father's sheep, because she was a shepherd."

I thought) muttered a word of thanks to the stranger who had risked serious injury, or even death, to save him from the same. The driver continued on his way, my date came back to me, took my hand, and we resumed our walk. The entire episode was over in less than two minutes. But, perhaps like Rachel when Jacob rolls the heavy stone from the well, I was impressed. A short incident offered a glimpse of what this man could do, and more insightfully, who he was. We have been married for over thirty years.

Perhaps because of this experience, which prompted feelings of kinship with Rachel, I thought for many years that the Rachel-Jacob story was an enchanting biblical romance. After he moves that heavy stone, Jacob kisses Rachel and weeps, apparently for his sheer love of her (Gen. 29:11). He explains their family connection (they're cousins!) by mentioning his mother, Rebekah, and Rachel runs and tells her father, Laban (v. 12).[12] Genesis 29:18 specifies that Jacob loved Rachel, giving a rare glimpse inside a biblical character's emotions. (In the Bible, as in life, we usually discern how people feel by what they say and do.) Does Rachel love him back? Does she feel cherished or attacked when Jacob kisses her? Does she run to her father because she is thrilled or terrified? Unless we hear her side of the story, we can't know. Sometimes a woman tells us her side of the story, but we ignore or deny or dismiss it (in the Bible and in life). Perhaps we're too used to tuning out women. But the women of Genesis cannot be entirely ignored because, in many ways, the Bible's story relies on them.

Jacob has children with four women/wives:[13] Leah and Rachel, and their maids, Zilpah and Bilhah; their offspring become the twelve tribes of Israel. In a remarkable scene, Leah and Rachel bargain for sexual rights to Jacob, who silently complies with their

12. While the idea of marrying your cousin seems unwise to us, endogamy or marrying within one's social group is encouraged in biblical texts. Clan and tribal endogamy persists in pastoral societies today where keeping flocks within the family is a priority. Marrying outside your community, clan, or tribe is called exogamy.

13. As in French (*la femme*), the same Hebrew word (*ishah*) means both "woman" and "wife."

wishes (Gen. 30:14–17). Along with his sons, Jacob has a daughter, Dinah, by Leah (see Gen. 34), and more unnamed daughters as well (37:35; 46:7, 15). The first of his many children has one of my favorite biblical names: Reuben, which means "Look! A son!" Once again, you might expect that the firstborn son of the father would come to prominence, but the mother has a key role in determining which child rises. Among all Jacob's children, beloved Rachel's older son, Joseph, becomes the star of the family story. Again, the role of the mother and her special child matter most.

Joseph, in some ways, reminds me of my own son, Graham. My daughter, Mari, first called my attention to this connection when she was taking a college literature class and the professor had assigned the book of Genesis.

"I think Joseph had Asperger's," Mari mentioned in one of her phone calls home.

"Why?" I asked. Even though I teach the Bible and my son is on the autism spectrum, I had not made any association.

"Well, Joseph is a visual thinker. He sees things differently from his brothers and has abilities that they don't, like interpreting dreams. But socially, he struggles."

Then I knew what she meant.

Among all Jacob's children, Joseph is the most beloved by his father. Both Joseph and Benjamin are borne by Jacob's cherished wife Rachel. Genesis 37:3 explains that Jacob prefers Joseph as "the son of his old age," but Benjamin comes after Joseph, when Jacob is even older (Gen. 30:22–24; 35:16–18). So why is Joseph the favorite? Perhaps Jacob focuses on Joseph because he realizes that his son needs more attention than his siblings. Jacob gives this special (needs?) son the famous coat of many colors. The Hebrew words for this garment are *ketonet passim*, perhaps best envisioned as a "striped gown" (v. 3; translation mine). While a garment with different colors might not seem especially impressive to us, in the ancient world multiple dyes derived from natural sources and hours of labor woven into one garment was a huge extravagance, especially among herding families like Jacob's (see v. 12). As a gown, the robe has sleeves, so it was not designed for field work, like the simple tunics nearly everyone wore all the time. Rather, Joseph wears the clothing of royalty; indeed, the only other time the words *ketonet passim* appear in the Bible they describe the dress of the princess Tamar, King David's daughter (2 Sam. 13:18). Jacob is marking Joseph for greatness, not with something expensive and small, like a jeweled ring, but with a flashy and distinct garment that is visible from a distance (see Gen. 37:18). Perhaps Jacob has observed that Joseph is different from his other children. Perhaps Jacob senses some vulnerability and wants to help Joseph by supporting him and even compensating for some of the challenges Joseph faces and the ostracism he sometimes endures.[14] I know the feeling.

Graham was diagnosed with Asperger's syndrome (or high-functioning autism, now called being "on the spectrum") when he was five years old.[15] Largely due to his lack of interest in other children, Graham's kindergarten teacher suggested that our son should be evaluated. A few weeks later, my husband and I met with the school psychologist in a cramped, windowless office for the assessment. He informed us that our son was "fine," even very bright. Graham knows the word "polite," the psychologist told us. "Polite?!" I replied. "Ask him what a herpetologist does." (Graham was interested in reptiles at the time.) We then went to another psychologist who ran further tests and informed us that our son had Asperger's, a form of autism. "Autism" can be a very scary word for a parent. Upon hearing of our son's diagnosis, a colleague who had an autistic son said to my husband and me,

14. For further discussion of Joseph and autism, see Levine, *Was Yosef on the Spectrum?*

15. Asperger's syndrome was first listed in the American Psychiatric Association's 1994 edition of *Diagnostic and Statistical Manual of Mental Disorders IV* (known as the DSM-4). In the more recent DSM-5 (2013), Asperger's syndrome has been replaced with the diagnosis of autism spectrum disorder (ASD), accompanied by numerical indications of severity.

"Welcome to the club that no one wants to join." Maybe he meant to be empathetic, but his words fell and festered in the pit of my stomach.

Perhaps like Jacob, my husband and I mustered resources to support our son. In some ways, like Joseph, the extra attention marked him as a target. Graham did not have an extravagant coat, but he was set apart in other ways, like being pulled out of class and having aides hovering around him during his school years. Perhaps like Jacob, I was well-intentioned, but sometimes my efforts were misguided, and my son bore the brunt of my wrong decisions. Joseph, like Graham, both benefited and suffered from his differences.[16] Joseph's brothers resent him so much that they plan to kill him (Gen. 37:18–20). But in the end, those same strange abilities that make Joseph's brothers so jealous are what save the lives of his family members and, indeed, the people of Israel (50:15–21). Those with special needs often bring special gifts.

Surging forward, figuring out how to get what you need, using other people, arguing over inheritances, feeling isolated, and experiencing parental favoritism, sibling rivalry, moments of intimacy, hurtful betrayal, lasting romance, times of fighting, solidarity, and bonding—family members in Genesis support and oppose each other through life's banes and blessings, just like the people in my family and yours.

I take great comfort from Genesis when I see how biblical families struggle, as I did at times while raising my son. These stories push aside idealized media-fueled notions about how flawless families should be and instead recognize that the grit of life is a gift. Through challenges, we learn and grow. Complicated biblical family dynamics help me to be just a little bit easier on myself. Cultural pressures on families (and especially mothers) to be perfect are unfair and oppressive. We try. We make mistakes.

---

16. While Graham can struggle socially, he has an extraordinary memory and ability to retain knowledge, especially about animals.

We try again. We move on, and hopefully learn a few things along the way. Just like our biblical ancestors.

So what's feminist about Genesis? Feminism, like its partner, love, is about acceptance and respect. Justice, or love with legs, is their child. Feminism helps women, me included, love ourselves enough to seek the rights that all people deserve. Similarly, Genesis values women through its portrayals of everyday, world-changing women whose lives and stories matter. These women have desires and dreams that they strive to realize. We glimpse their successes and failures in portrayals of families that aren't concerned with being cheerful and well-groomed or having tidily resolved their issues.

Instead, Genesis depicts families as those with whom we dare to share our raw, honest selves. The people closest to us know the neediness oozing from our pores and love us anyway, which is what makes them family. The Bible's unfolding drama of God's involvement with humanity starts with families, where our own life stories begin. Genesis affirms that you and I have a place in this drama of God's expanding action revealed in the everyday messes that we are. We originate in families, the experimental living laboratories of God's love.

-------- **Questions for Reflection and Conversation** --------

1. What does "family" mean to you? How have those whom you consider family contributed to the person you are?

2. Abraham and Sarah leave their homeland, and their lives are forever changed. What transition in your life changed your story significantly?

3. When has someone come to help you in your time of need, like an angel sent by God? When have you been an angel or a messenger of God's love for someone else? Who brings you comfort or leads you toward joy?

Sex Workers, Slaughters, and Deities without Borders

When I teach my students the historical books of Joshua through Kings, I hand out Tootsie Pops. Holding up an unwrapped sticky red globe on its small white stick, I ask them to imagine tasting this sweet treat for the first time. A few minutes after putting the round lollipop in their mouths, they detect the squishy tootsie roll in the middle; the candy is more interesting. I explain that the chocolate centers in Tootsie Pops are like the goddesses and prostitutes in the Bible. Surprise! Usually, we barely stop to notice them—but when we do, our experience (of tasting or reading) suddenly becomes more intriguing.

Part of the Bible's appeal is its ability to pull us into its captivating stories with people and plots that we would never expect. A history that seems straightforward brims with unlikely characters whom God uses in astounding ways. Theology develops through collected stories about resilient believers that end up (oh yeah) changing the history of humanity.

History and theology are intertwined in the Bible. This close connection is perhaps most apparent in the books of Joshua, Judges, 1 and 2 Samuel, and 1 and 2 Kings, which tell of Israel's growth and development from a tribal people to a nation-state. A unifying theme throughout these books comes from Deuteronomy: do not worship gods or goddesses besides Yahweh.[1] Even the first of the Ten Commandments points to their presence: "I am the LORD your God. . . . You shall have no other gods before me" (Exod. 20:2–3; Deut. 5:6–7).[2] That's *God* admitting to other gods and saying, in effect, "Sure, other gods exist, just be sure to choose me over them." My students rarely think about other deities mentioned in the Bible besides God, but the *Dictionary of Deities and Demons in the Bible* lists hundreds of them.[3]

Most believers I know have faith that angels exist and do not give much attention to demons. But Jesus interacts with both kinds of otherworldly beings, some of whom talk with him (Matt. 8:31; Mark 1:34; Luke 4:41; 8:30–32). Do we think we know the spiritual world better than Jesus does?

---

1. Scholars use the term "Deuteronomistic History" to indicate the literary unit comprising Joshua, Judges, 1 and 2 Samuel, and 1 and 2 Kings. Ruth comes after Judges in Christian Bibles because it begins with the words, "In the days when the judges ruled . . .". However, Ruth is not part of the Deuteronomistic History because it is a short story about a family, not a continued account of Israel's history.

2. In English Bibles "the LORD" is written in capital letters when the Hebrew gives the four letters יהוה (*yod, heh, vav, heh*), which signify God's name. Together they are known as the tetragrammaton (Greek for "four letters"). The letters יהוה are transliterated as YHWH and pronounced (by Christians) as "Yahweh." Jews do not speak God's proper name out loud but instead usually say "Adonai" when the text provides YHWH. (In this book, "the LORD" is in all caps when I am quoting a printed translation.)

3. *The Dictionary of Deities and Demons in the Bible* (edited by van der Toorn, Becking, and van der Horst) discusses all the gods, goddesses, and demons found in the Hebrew Bible, Apocrypha, and New Testament, with a total list of close to six hundred entries.

Once I had a strange experience that might be explained as an interaction with demonic power. I was in New Orleans for a conference and decided to explore the tourist scene. Along with a few colleagues, I was strolling down the famous Bourbon Street, where locals with baskets of beads stand on the Spanish balconies of the Creole townhouses that line the street. When a woman looks up and lifts her shirt, those on the balconies throw down beads (hardly a feminist practice, but you need to choose your battles). A male colleague of mine with a playful disposition, Keith, lifted the shirt he was wearing and down came a string of pink, shiny beads. He caught them and, not being interested in pink (even color is gendered in our highly binary world!), gave them to me. I later shared them with my friend and conference roommate, Lin, as an accessory for the sharp black Ann Taylor dress she was wearing. None of these actions was unusual for a day in New Orleans—but the night was scarily strange.

Both Lin and I had horrific nightmares. I dreamed that a close friend was being thrown from a tower to her death (no kidding—just like Jezebel in 2 Kings 9:30–37). I screamed out loud in my sleep, which I had never done before, and Lin woke me up. She had also been having a nightmare and described a haunting image of two dirt-encrusted coffins that were lifted from underneath our beds and placed on top of them.

"I have a feeling that two people killed themselves in this hotel room," she told me.

"Why did we both have such awful dreams?" I asked her.

Lin didn't hesitate: "It's the beads."

I cannot know if she was right, but I do know that she threw them away the next day and for the rest of the conference, we slept just fine.

People in the modern world may or may not believe in demons or angels or God or any god, but people in the biblical world did. In the ancient Near East, saying that you did not believe in gods would be like saying today that you do not believe in air. If someone told you that they thought there was no air, you might ask them how that strategy worked, denying air's existence. Is that even an option? People in antiquity knew gods existed with the conviction that we have regarding air: this invisible reality keeps you alive. While we obviously cannot see air, we nonetheless observe its effects in ourselves and in the world around us (filling lungs, blowing through trees, raising waves, etc.). Similarly, the ancients could not see actual gods and goddesses but could recognize their effects in themselves and in the world around them (enabling conception, sending rain, granting military victory, etc.). The deities that people worshiped were largely determined by place of origin. Allegiance to particular gods and goddesses was fierce, kind of like the fanatical devotion that many people today feel for the sports teams from their hometown.

The best-known god of the Canaanites (the people of the wider region where Israel is found) was Baal, who is mentioned around ninety times in the Old Testament. He was the weather/rain/fertility god of the region. You may have heard of him. The most famous of the Canaanite goddesses is Asherah; the Old Testament contains about forty references to her or to the symbol of a sacred tree that is associated with worshiping her. She was the mother goddess of the Canaanite pantheon. Have you ever heard of her?

Asherah was popular in the region of the Israelites. The Bible does not give us her portfolio, although goddesses in the ancient Near East held a range of responsibilities, including protecting cities, inventing writing, fighting wars, ruling the underworld, reigning in the heavens, and inciting love (not just fertility!). Part of the reason that you likely are not familiar with Asherah stems from translators' choices. Of the forty times that the word *asherah* appears in the Bible, the translation that appears over thirty times in the NRSV is "sacred pole." Other translators render *asherah* as "grove" (KJV), "wooden post" (NKJV), and "sacred post" (NJPS). Perhaps the most helpful translation comes from the NIV, which translates *asherah* as "Asherah pole" and explains in a note that this is "a wooden symbol of the goddess Asherah." Yet for the most part, translators collude with Bible writers to downplay the presence of the region's best-known goddess by erasing or obscuring references to her. Even Bibles that straightforwardly render the Hebrew *asherah* as "Asherah" still leave many Bible readers confused. "Who's Asherah?" "What's an asherah?"

Yet Asherah was so well-known in the biblical world that she cannot entirely be pushed aside.[4] The Bible repeatedly testifies to her power. References to the goddess or her sacred tree symbol show that she was known by royalty and in the capital cities (1 Kings 15:13; 18:19; 2 Kings 13:6; 23:4–7). People in the towns as well as the countryside set up symbols of devotion to her (Judg. 6:25–30; 1 Kings 14:22–23; 2 Kings 17:9–10). Deuteronomy 16:21 instructs followers of Yahweh not to put an *asherah* symbol next to God's altar, inadvertently showing a cultic connection between the two deities. This relationship is evidenced further by two famous inscriptions that link the God of the Hebrew Bible to "his Asherah."[5] Susan Ackerman notes, "Archaeological discoveries from the later 1970s and early 1980s have further indicated that at least in the opinion of some ancient Israelites, YHWH and Asherah were appropriately worshipped as a pair."[6]

We might think it strange to acknowledge the possibility of gods or goddesses other than God in the Bible, much less in our own lives, but many of us may be closer to goddess worship than we realize. Those who venerate Mary probably do not think of her as a goddess, but having a home shrine with a small statue

4. For further discussion of Asherah and other goddesses in the Bible, see "Goddesses of the Hebrew Bible and Ugaritic Literature" on p. 137 in chapter 10 of this book.

5. An inscription is writing on a hard surface, such as stone or pottery. One inscription on a pottery jar dates from the eighth century BCE and was found at Kuntillet Ajrud, a site in the northeast part of the Sinai Peninsula. This writing refers to "Yahweh and his Asherah." Another inscription from around the same time was found in Khirbet el-Qom, the modern-day West Bank, and also pairs Yahweh with Asherah.

6. Ackerman, "Asherah/Asherim," 510. See also Dever, *Did God Have a Wife?*

of a female figure whom you pray to and praise closely mirrors ancient practices of goddess worship. Who knew?

I am not Roman Catholic, so attention to Mary and the saints was not a focus in my spiritual upbringing. In recent years, however, I have become an adoring fan (devotee?) of Saint Anthony, who is known for retrieving lost objects. When looking for a misplaced item, I silently call on Saint Anthony and ask for help. Then I think hard about the whereabouts of the lost object. Often I receive a vision of where to find it and voilà—a few minutes later, what was lost is found. Try it sometime. While this approach is not guaranteed, it is effective enough to amaze me. Once I lost a necklace that I loved, yet I did not fret because I happened to be in San Antonio, Texas, a city named for my favorite saint, where I knew his power must be strong. Within minutes of realizing that I had lost my necklace, I received a text from a woman whom I had met only once telling me that she had found my necklace, which she then mailed to my home. Talk about Anthony in a show-offy mood!

People in the biblical world needed their gods and goddesses to be in a show-offy mood nearly all the time because survival was so challenging. About half of children born did not live to age fifteen.[7] Children who did manage to grow into adults generally lived only into their thirties.[8] Complications in childbirth, wounds from warfare, starvation from famine, festering infections, rampant plagues, lethal diseases—any one of these deadly erasers could smudge you out of the picture. People needed deities with *power*. The Hebrew Bible offers tales of conquest and victory for the Israelites because they were surrounded by aggressive world empires, with Mesopotamia to the east and Egypt to the west. Fabulous, faith-fostering stories about a mighty, miraculous God delivering this chosen community from enemies would encourage

7. Garroway, *Growing Up in Ancient Israel*, 223–24.
8. For detailed discussion, see Eng, *Days of Our Years*, 38–44.

people to believe in Yahweh instead of the competing deities without borders.

One of these conquest stories celebrates the triumph of Joshua and the battle of Jericho (Josh. 6). God instructs the Israelites to march around Jericho for seven days, led by seven priests blowing seven trumpets. On the final day, the priests blast their horns one long, loud, last time, the people shout, and the monumental city's walls crash into ruins (or "came tumblin' down," as the spiritual goes). Did you also know that the story ends in slaughter and starts with a sex worker?

Joshua 2 introduces Rahab, a prostitute who hides the Israelite spies who come to scout out Jericho before invading the land of Canaan. When the king of Jericho orders Rahab to give up the spies, she deceives him with the classic cartoon move "They went thataway!" sending the pursuers on a wild goose chase. In return, the scouts promise to save Rahab and her family when the Israelites come back later to (oh yeah) obliterate her town and her people.

Lori Rowlett offers a compelling comparison between Rahab and Disney's *Pocahontas*.[9] I remember seeing *Pocahontas* in the movie theater, sitting next to my children as we shared a tub of greasy popcorn and slurped sugary Cokes. We stared up at the screen, enraptured by the colorful animation and catchy music, as the gorgeous, busty Native American woman aided the colonists and fell helplessly in love with the dashingly handsome John Smith. Disney conveniently brushes aside those annoying historical details of germ warfare and genocide to offer a fable of a romance that bridged cultural divides. Rowlett compares Rahab to this portrayal of Pocahontas, noting that both highly sexualized women instantly side with the invaders *over their own people*. In Joshua 2:9–11, Rahab gives a speech about the power of the Israelite God. She even cites incidents from Hebrew Scripture (has

9. Rowlett, "Disney's Pocahontas and Joshua's Rahab in Postcolonial Perspective."

she been studying Torah between clients?).[10] In Disney's *Poca-hontas*, the heroine risks her life to save John Smith. He and his cohort have journeyed to this lush continent to steal land and resources and kill anyone who gets in the way (although the movie, of course, never dwells on this reality). Yet, like Rahab, Pocahontas defends the invader, and we, the readers/movie-goers, never question her allegiance. The unspoken understanding is that the exotic foreign woman would naturally help the dominating male because of his presumed inherent superiority. The controlling narrator/filmmaker effectively guides our thinking into valorizing male conquest.

Patriarchy rewards women who enforce its values; Rahab and Pocahontas survive. But most of their people are slaughtered.[11] Biblical stories of such brutal killing prompt some Christians to declare, "The God of the Old Testament is a God of war, but the God of the New Testament is a God of love." But who is the God of Jesus, a Jew named after Joshua? The God of the Old Testament is also known for steadfast love and liberating mercy. And Jesus is not all sunshine and puppies (e.g., Matt. 10:21, 34–35; Luke 12:53).

The Hebrew Scriptures, which are Jesus' Scriptures, offer the start of an ongoing connection with God—a crucial sliver, a crack of light. What distinguishes this specific God, Yahweh, from others in antiquity is God's strong desire to be in relationship with human beings. God adopts a group of people, the Israelites, who later become known as the Jews, and loves them. For Christians, this love becomes incarnate in one of these Jews named Jesus. For Jews, God's love is manifest in the Torah of beloved teachings. The Scriptures of both Jews and Christians share the same theo-

---

10. Compare Josh. 2:10 with Exod. 14:29 and Deut. 3:1–7.

11. For documentation of the Bible's role in the killing of Native Americans, see Mato Nunpa, *Great Evil*. In the Bible, all the Canaanites of Jericho are destroyed by sword: "men and women, young and old, oxen, sheep, and donkeys" (Josh. 6:21); only Rahab's family is spared (6:22–25).

logical foundation. Jesus highlights this central belief as he quotes the Torah, telling his followers to love the Lord with all that they are (Matt. 22:37; Mark 12:30; Luke 10:27a; cf. Deut. 6:5) and to love their neighbors as themselves (Mark 12:31; Matt. 22:39; Luke 10:27b; cf. Lev. 19:18). The Bible is our *introduction* to the God who loves us, not the conclusion. Nothing can limit the love of God, *not even the Bible.* And God's love extends equally to everyone.

Perhaps the Bible has so many unlikely heroes to remind us that God loves and works through all kinds of people, including everyday characters who are often overshadowed by the outstanding ones.

One of the most beloved stories of the historical books tells of King Solomon resolving a dispute between two women fighting over the same baby (1 Kings 3:16–28). They lived together and gave birth within three days of each other. When one woman accidentally smothered her child while he slept, she switched her own dead son for the other mother's living son. The women come before Solomon, and each claims that the living baby is hers. Solomon hears their complaints and requests a sword to divide the remaining child and give each woman half. At this point, the mother of the living baby implores Solomon to give the other woman the child instead of killing him "because compassion for her son burned within her" (v. 26).[12] The second woman agrees to chop the infant in half! In his infinite (obvious?) wisdom, Solomon announces that the woman who wants to keep the child alive is the real mother and that she should be given the baby. All of Israel stands in awe of the king's judgment.

A rarely mentioned detail of this well-known story is that both women are prostitutes. The Hebrew reads *nashim zonot* (1 Kings 3:16), the plural of *ishah zonah*, the word used to describe Rahab

---

12. The Hebrew word for "compassion" in this verse, *rakhamim*, means "a feeling of love, loving sensation, mercy" and is derived from the word *rekhem*, meaning "womb." Koehler, Baumgartner, and Stamm, *Hebrew and Aramaic Lexicon*, 1218, 1217.

(Josh. 2:1). The word *ishah* means "woman" and *zonah* indicates sex outside of marriage.

What difference does it make, I ask my students, that the women before Solomon are sex workers?

"Their occupation explains why they live together."

"The women need to speak for themselves. They don't have husbands."

"Solomon cares for *everyone* in his kingdom."

To these answers, I add another possibility: "The baby may be the woman's only family," an insight I gained through working with prostitutes.

While in seminary, I had a part-time position at a shelter for homeless women with children located on West Forty-Sixth Street in Manhattan. Today this area—Times Square—is like Disney-world north, as family-friendly costumed characters overcharge tourists for photos in front of neon-drenched urban scenery. But back then, this famed region of the city stank of garbage and danger, littered with dirty needles and lurid sex shops. Anne, a few months pregnant, and her two-year-old son, Dustin, stepped off a Greyhound bus into *this* Times Square, having fled from Georgia and the pointed gun of Anne's abusive husband. A police officer at the Port Authority station directed this overwhelmed pregnant mother and her young child to the shelter, where we met.

My first day there was also hers and the director of the shelter paired us up. I was to support this petite, Southern, strawberry-blonde woman as she and her towheaded son adjusted to their new surroundings. Together Anne and I learned about life in this shelter. Together we walked around the neighborhood when we needed a short respite. Together we sat in the overcrowded waiting room at Bellevue hospital for six hours before her prenatal appointment. We grew closer as the weeks passed and her stomach got bigger. I told my mother, Merolyn, about Anne. While not a rich woman, my mother was generous without boundaries. She invited Anne and Dustin to live with her and my father on Long

Island as the impending birth approached. Grateful for relief from the unrelenting stress of the shelter, Anne accepted immediately. She and Dustin shared my former bedroom.

The tragic element in this otherwise heartwarming story, as is so often the case, was drugs. After Anne had been living in my parents' home for a few weeks, my mother started finding used syringes in the bathroom. We came to discover that Anne was addicted to heroin and prostituting herself to pay for her habit. Anne would say she was going into the city to pick up her welfare check and not come back to the house on Long Island for two weeks, leaving my working parents to juggle constant childcare for Dustin. I was still in denial. "She can't be prostituting herself," I protested to my supervisor at the shelter. "She's eight months pregnant!" My experienced boss sighed, shook her head, and placed her hand on my forearm. "Honey, you've got a lot to learn."

Anne gave birth on Christmas Eve. Directly after the 11 p.m. worship service, my mother and I drove to the county hospital and visited her in the maternity ward. "I do one thing well," Anne said with an exhausted smile. "I make beautiful babies." She was right. The infant was adorable: chubby cheeks, big blue eyes, and a shock of dark hair. But he was not hers to keep. Anne put the baby up for adoption as an act of compassionate womb-love. And indeed, that little boy grew up with parents who cherished him as the joy of their world.

Anne's story both clarifies and complicates the biblical story of Solomon and the prostitutes in 1 Kings 3:16–28. This story reads like a fairy tale: the "once upon a time" opening, the conflict between good and evil embodied through the women, and the resolution facilitated by the powerful man who enables the "happily ever after" ending.[13] Anne was like the mother plead-

13. For example, Cinderella must deal with her "evil stepmother" and stepsisters and is rescued by Prince Charming; Snow White is threatened by her "evil stepmother" and is rescued by Prince Charming; Sleeping Beauty is put to temporary death by a "wicked witch" and comes to life by a kiss from Prince Charming.

ing to Solomon, who loved her baby so much she was willing to hand him over to another mother. In Anne's story, the adoptive parents, last I heard, got their happy ending in beginning a life with their son. Yet for Anne, the persistent pain of poverty and addiction did not magically disappear when she gave her newborn to the caring couple. Dustin went to live with his grandmother, who raised him. The last time I saw Anne she was in a prison in Georgia, where she was serving time for forging checks. Two years later, she died of AIDS.

To understand Anne as a "bad" prostitute—a drug addict who robbed people of their hard-earned money—would be easy. Yet her story is more complicated—she suffered abuse, and she tried to care for her children, even when that care required the womb-love sacrifice of letting them go. Quick categorizations of people, especially women, can be seductive and destructive.

Feminism invites us to question common representations of women in opposition, like the selfish/altruistic prostitutes: Eve/Mary, whore/virgin, evil stepmother/virtuous maiden, nagging shrew/happy housewife, bitchy boss/eager ingenue, and so on. As with all stereotypes, these portrayals steal power from the labeled person, who becomes typecast and is discounted and dismissed as "one of those." Who is served in such scenarios? Of course, scenes of women clawing each other ("cat fights") provide juicy drama. Imagine if 2 Kings 3:16–17 read like this: "Two women who were prostitutes came and stood before the king. One woman said, 'Please my lord, this woman and I live in the same house. We both gave birth three days apart from each other. Then she accidentally smothered her child in her sleep, so I comforted her, and we have become even closer as a result of this terrible loss.'" Where's the action? What's at stake?

People's lives are at stake in the ways we read and understand the Bible. All too often, Scripture can be wielded as a weapon that denigrates, demeans, and even destroys people just for being who they are. Stories of Joshua's conquests, for example, were used to justify torture and murder of Native peoples by European invaders to the Americas.[14] God-sanctioned genocide? God help us.

The Bible—our confounding, cherished, challenging introduction to God—does help us by broadening our theological horizons. Goddesses in the Bible, with Asherah often accompanying Yahweh? A Torah-knowledgeable Canaanite sex worker as the hero? Two prostitutes acting like lawyers? Scenes of slaughter do not *prescribe* what we should do but *describe* how a struggling band of Yahweh-loving people imagined their God granting them dramatic victories. They told these stories to stay alive as a people of faith. The appalling irony is that these same stories have been used to kill people of other faiths.

We can justify our actions and attitudes—for good or evil—with the Bible. But the behavior you or I seek to rationalize says more about us than it does about God's very varied word. When we use (read: abuse) biblical texts to destroy other peoples or deny any person their full humanity, whose will do we reflect? The God of the Bible or the God of our bombast?

The Bible weaves together imagination, truth, memory, fantasy, trauma, joy, history, and theology so tightly that the strands become hard to distinguish. The question is not so much "Did this really happen?" but "What truths are there for me in this passage? What can I learn from this story through deeper investigation? How do I embrace or resist this text to affirm God's will for love and life?" Sex workers, slaughters, and deities without borders shake up our rigid, moralistic assumptions about the Bible, broadening our understanding of the biblical world, and, by reflection, our own.

---

14. For a succinct and horrific historical account of how biblical texts were used to encourage the torture and annihilation of Native peoples, see Mato Nunpa, "Sweet-Smelling Sacrifice."

---- **Questions for Reflection and Conversation** ----

1. The Bible writers told stories about stunning Israelite victories to impart strength to the tribes of people who shared their beliefs. What story about your own life or that of your family do you like to tell? What does this story convey about you or your family?

2. Stereotypes put people into categories that have little, if anything, to do with their actual lives. At first glance, how might someone size you up? How accurate, if at all, would their perception be?

3. What do you believe in that you cannot see? Where do your beliefs come from? Why do you hold on to them?

Profit from Prophecy

The voice on the other side of the wall was so loud that my husband and I needed to rearrange our bedroom furniture. The words we heard in the middle of the night, usually intelligible but sometimes not, were coming from my father while he slept. He moved in with my family when my mother suddenly died. Living in close proximity confirmed what I had suspected for years: my father was a prophet. From my Old Testament studies, I had come to realize that prophets went far beyond the portrait of bearded white guys with flowing robes, fiery eyes, and holier-than-thou authority. Rather, a wide range of people in the Bible are prophets, and even today prophets can be found all around us, if we just know how to look for them.

Fifteen books clustered together in the Bible dominate our conventional thinking about who prophets are and what they do. The first group of these prophetic books—Isaiah, Jeremiah, and Ezekiel—are known as the major prophets. They are called "major" not due to their messages or influence but simply because their books are longer than those of the twelve "minor" prophets (Hosea, Joel, Amos, Obadiah, Jonah, Micah, Nahum, Habakkuk,

Zephaniah, Haggai, Zechariah, and Malachi).[1] Together, Isaiah through Malachi form the corpus of writing prophets, with books that bear these men's names. The writings of the major prophets combine poetry and prose. The writings of the minor prophets consist mostly of prophetic speeches, with a few exceptions, especially among the later books.[2] Called into service, the prophets share messages from God. While our Bibles say "the word of the Lord 'came'" to the prophets, the Hebrew reads *vayehi devar Yahweh*: "the word of the Lord 'fell upon' [the prophet]" or "the word of the Lord 'happened' [to the prophet]." God drafts prophets to respond to the political situations of their day. As the leaders and people tried to cope with threats of approaching invaders or recover from onslaughts of war, messages from God came through these prophets to warn, scold, guide, and uphold a rightfully frightened people.

In addition to these fifteen men, more prophets, including women, are found throughout the Bible.[3] In the New Testament, the Greek word for prophet means "one who speaks forth" and can designate a man (*prophētēs*) or a woman (*prophētis*). The most common Hebrew word for a prophet in the Old Testament is *navi* (masc.) or *neviah* (fem.), associated with the Akkadian verb *nabu*, meaning "to call." Prophets are called *by* the deity and also call people *to* that deity. In the Greco-Roman world and throughout the ancient Near East, both women and men functioned as prophets.[4] Indeed, in the Mesopotamian empire of Neo-Assyria, which

1. The collection of minor prophets is called "the Book of the Twelve" in Jewish tradition, since all these books could fit on one scroll. Christian tradition also includes Daniel among the prophets.

2. Jonah is a narrated story. The books of Haggai, Zechariah, and Malachi consist mostly of prose, offering sermons, visions, and judgments, respectively.

3. For references to girls and women described as prophets or portrayed using prophetic gifts, see Exod. 15:20; Judg. 4:4; 1 Sam. 28:7; 2 Kings 22:14; Isa. 8:3; Ezek. 13:17–32; Joel 2:28; Neh. 6:14; Luke 2:36; Acts 2:17–18; 16:16; 21:9; 1 Cor. 11:5; and Rev. 2:20. For discussion of female prophets in the Hebrew Bible, as well as in rabbinic and Christian traditions, see Gafney, *Daughters of Miriam*.

4. For detailed discussion, see Nissinen, *Ancient Prophecy*, 297–324.

existed at the time of the events recorded in many Old Testament texts, female prophets significantly outnumber male prophets.[5] The Bible is unusual in its cultural context in that it records relatively few women prophets, yet even in this androcentric text, some emerge to fulfill essential religious roles.

The longest biblical story of a female prophet belongs to Deborah—the commander and military leader who judged Israel before this tribal society had a king (Judg. 4–5). She is introduced as an *ishah neviah* (woman prophet) and *eshet lappidoth*, which is usually translated as "the wife of Lappidoth" (4:4). However, no person named "Lappidoth" appears anywhere else in the Bible, and this name is strange for a man since it has a feminine plural ending (*-oth*). The Hebrew word *lappid* means "torch" and *eshet* can be translated as "woman" or "wife."[6] Deborah's description as an *eshet lappidoth* suggests a fiery woman, perhaps like Xena from the *Warrior Princess* television series or Katniss Everdeen in the movie *The Hunger Games*. Like these heroic figures, Deborah is fearless and valiant. She expands the traditional view of a prophet as she is sought as an accomplice in war (vv. 4–10) and credited for bringing prosperity as "a mother in Israel" (5:7). At the same time, Deborah fulfills an established prophetic role in correctly predicting the future, here foretelling the outcome of an impending battle: "The Lord will sell Sisera [the enemy] into the power of a woman" (4:9; translation mine). And indeed, Israelite victory comes through a woman (vv. 17–24).

Like Deborah, Huldah is a woman to whom men turn for guidance. In 2 Kings 22:3–20, King Josiah of Judah orders repairs to the Jerusalem temple, which results in the high priest, Hilkiah,

---

5. Stökl and Carvalho, *Prophets Male and Female*, 3.

6. The plural of *lappid* is *lappidim* meaning "torches" (Judg. 7:16, 20; 15:4–5; Job 41:19 [MT: 41:11]; Ezek. 1:13; Dan. 10:6; Nah. 2:4 [MT: 2:5]). (The abbreviation MT stands for "Masoretic Text" and designates the Hebrew Bible that is the basis for translations.) Deborah is explicitly described as a "woman of flames" in rabbinic literature. See Gafney, *Daughters of Miriam*, 188n42.

finding a scroll. When Josiah first hears the document's contents, he is anguished because Yahweh's laws have not been followed, and he instructs his counselors to "inquire of the LORD" (v. 13).[7] A parade of powerful men of the palace—Hilkiah; Shaphan the scribe and his son Ahikam; Achbor, son of Micaiah; and Asaiah, the king's servant—seek out the prophet Huldah (vv. 11–14). Interestingly, Jeremiah is a prophet residing in the same region at the time of Josiah.[8] Why don't the kings' advisers turn to him? Perhaps these men prefer Huldah's prophetic guidance since Jeremiah was critical of kings (e.g., Jer. 4:9; 13:18). Like Isaiah (e.g., Isa. 7; 37), Huldah appears to function as a court prophet, consulted by royalty. Using the classic phrase of prophetic utterance, "Thus says the Lord" (*koh amar* Y~HWH~), Huldah correctly predicts Jerusalem's destruction, while assuring Josiah that his own humility has saved him from disaster (2 Kings 22:15–20). However, the text later reports that Josiah is killed by Pharaoh Neco and is brought back—dead—in his chariot to Jerusalem (23:29–30). The contrast between this violent account of Josiah's death and Huldah's prediction of his peaceful end may suggest that the tradition surrounding her role as a prophet was strong. The Bible retained her story without later adjustment, despite conflicting reports.[9]

Also in the vanguard of her people and their politics, Miriam, sister of Moses and Aaron, is called a prophet (Exod. 15:20). As a girl, she helps to rescue baby Moses from a watery grave (2:1–10). When grown, she leads Israelite women with songs and dancing to celebrate the crossing of the Red Sea and the liberation from

7. The Hebrew verb *darash*, here translated as "inquire," typically appears when someone seeks divine insight. See also the story of the medium from Endor (1 Sam. 28:7), as well as numerous prophetic texts (e.g., Isa. 31:1; 34:16; 55:6; 58:2; 65:10; Jer. 21:2; 29:7; Ezek. 20:1; Hosea 10:12; Amos 5:4–6; and Zeph. 1:6, among others).

8. Jeremiah came from Anathoth, a village about three miles northeast of Jerusalem. Jeremiah 1:1–2 relates that the word of the Lord "happened" to Jeremiah in the thirteenth year of Josiah's reign. Jeremiah's prophetic career extends to the Babylonian exile (Jer. 1:3), clearly including the eighteenth year of Josiah's reign, when the king seeks prophetic insight from Huldah (2 Kings 22:3). See also Jer. 3:6.

9. See Stökl, "Deborah, Huldah, and Innibana," 331.

slavery to freedom (15:20–21). Later Miriam, along with Aaron, claims her role as one who speaks on behalf of God (Num. 12:2). Her birth is listed in genealogies (26:59; 1 Chron. 6:3), and her death and burial are also chronicled (Num. 20:1). Miriam becomes one of the few remarkable biblical characters with four stages of life attested in the text: birth, childhood, adulthood, and death (a story from childhood being the hardest to find). Later prophetic tradition recalls her role in Israel's redemption (Mic. 6:4). Perhaps we should not be surprised that the authority of Miriam—a prominent religious leader—is challenged.

Numbers 12:1–15 shows Miriam, Aaron, Moses, and God in conflict. When Miriam and Aaron question the exclusivity of their brother Moses' role as prophet, the Lord comes down in a pillar of cloud. God explains that, to Moses, God speaks *peh el peh*, literally, "mouth to mouth" (not "face to face," as many English Bible translations read), suggesting a stunning (shocking?) intimacy (v. 8). God is furious with both Miriam and Aaron for challenging Moses as God's chosen prophet, but only Miriam becomes leprous, her skin as white and scaly as snow. Both Aaron and Moses make appeals on her behalf. But in a graphic and enigmatic rebuke, the Lord speaks of Miriam being spat on by her father and demands that she complete seven days of exile outside of the community (v. 14). Aaron receives no admonishment. Miriam's power may have been threatening to writers who felt she was too much on par with her brother, the high priest Aaron. The text tries hard to hold on to male control. What are feminists to do with such a story?

Finding affirmation for women's authority in Numbers 12 is not easy—but look closely. First, perhaps despite the writers' intentions, the Bible reveals that Miriam is not only a prophet but also a highly respected community leader along with Moses and Aaron, otherwise her role would not merit attention. Second, both Moses and Aaron, two of the Hebrew Bible's most famous characters, serve as her advocates. Aaron seems heartbroken to see his sister suffer (vv. 11–12). Moses cries out (*yetsaq*) and bravely commands God to heal her (*refa na lah*) (v. 13), taking risks on behalf of the sister who helped save his life as an infant. Third, the people of the community must care deeply about Miriam since they remain in place during her seven days of banishment and only move when she is again among them (vv. 15–16). For many women who are religious leaders, verses questioning Miriam's authority reflect a challenge they also face. They are denied positions and titles, not because they are unworthy or unable to fulfill responsibilities but due to entrenched gender-based ideas about leadership.

Biases against women as religious leaders stubbornly persist. I was ordained in the United Methodist Church when I was in my twenties, and at that time female ministers were relatively uncommon. In the congregation I served as a young pastor, a few people pulled me aside and confided, "I've never met one before." Feigning ignorance, I'd ask incredulously, "A woman who's five four with brown hair?" Then they would specify: "No, a lady minister [*sic*]!" These members considered me an oddity, almost a curiosity—not a person called by God like my male colleagues. Years later when I was working on my PhD, friends from a conservative church told me that their pastor was going on sabbatical and the congregation needed guest ministers to give the sermons on Sundays. "I'd gladly come preach," I told them, "but you won't allow my kind in your pulpit." Imagine if I had said that as an Asian person or as a black person or as a person in a wheelchair. Such blatant discrimination would not be tolerated. But as a woman? "Oh, our congregation is *traditional*" is a familiar refrain. Does that word become a veil for prejudice? Why do we still accept such reasoning as justified by the Bible when the Bible itself depicts strong women leaders in religious and political contexts?

As they predict the future (Deborah), advise royalty (Huldah), and lead their community (Miriam), these women illustrate some of the roles that prophets fulfill as divine-human intermediaries. Sociological studies describe various prophetic functions, including as seers (who have visions), priests (who function liturgically), preachers (who deliver God-inspired messages), mystics (who practice otherworldly devotion), diviners (who discern a deity's will), shamans (who channel spiritual power), mediums (who communicate with the dead), and wonder workers (who perform miracles). Anthropological studies highlight how different types of prophets function in cultures around the globe. In the biblical world, the structure of the natural world is perceived through senses, experience, and belief, intertwining what we understand as science, magic, and religion. Yet in modern, Western societies, we wear invisible post-Enlightenment blinders that limit our vision to seeing and accepting only phenomena that are rational and scientific. When healing takes place through a medical provider, such as a doctor or a surgeon, we accept this process as the result of abilities, training, and skill. But when healing takes place through a spiritual figure, such as a shaman or a wonder worker, we are skeptical of the process as the result of abilities, training, and skill. In exploring the biblical world, we need to expand our imaginations as to what is possible in the ways the world works.

When I teach my students about prophecy, I ask if they have ever witnessed or experienced an event that appears illogical. To get them started, I offer two brief personal stories. One night, years ago, my sleeping father loudly proclaimed, "Alida dies!" His voice woke up my husband (even with the rearranged furniture), who glanced at the clock: 4 a.m. The next morning we found out that my grandmother, Alida, had died at 4 a.m. Another odd occurrence happened at my aunt's funeral. Throughout the burial service, a red-tailed hawk stood still on the ground just outside the circle of mourners, its focus steady on the coffin. My son, who was twelve at the time, matter-of-factly informed me that the bird was the spirit of my aunt. This second story spurs my students' thinking.

Recollections tumble forth. One student shared a story with the class about her younger sister who died as a baby. A small white butterfly flew around the head of each immediate family member during the outside memorial service. "Whenever we have a family celebration, someone sees a small, white butterfly. If we're at a barbeque together, inevitably one flutters by. It's the weirdest thing," she told us. Another student talked about his mother dying in her forties from cancer. "Every year on her birthday, a rabbit sits still by the rosebush she planted in the garden." Someone else told about her toddler cousin who had managed to climb up to the top of a bunk bed. The moment my student entered the bedroom, the small boy was falling from the high bunk, but it seemed as if he was invisibly caught before landing safely and softly on the floor. "It was like he had been held for a moment by angels," she marveled. Over the years, I have heard lots of stories like these, and many can be categorized into two genres: animals witnessing to the spirit of a dead person and falling babies who remain unharmed.

The Bible abounds with stories that defy logic, including an intriguing account of the medium at Endor speaking with a dead person (1 Sam. 28:3–25).[10] Like Josiah when he discovers the scroll and has his advisers consult with Huldah, King Saul needs guidance and turns to a woman. The fearsome Philistine army is about to attack Saul's Israelite troops, and Saul wants to get advice from the prophet Samuel, who has died.[11] Saul's servants

---

10. While modern editors frequently insert "witch of Endor" as a heading above this story, the Hebrew term for "witch" (*mekhashepah*) does not appear in this passage. Indeed, the Hebrew calls her *baalat ov*, literally: "lord [fem., lowercase *l*] medium" (1 Sam. 28:7), granting a title of prestige. Some passages condemn practices outside traditional worship of Yahweh, like seeking consultation from the dead (Lev. 19:31; 20:6, 27), but other texts, like this story of the woman of Endor, testify to their efficacy.

11. Having fallen out of favor with Yahweh, Saul finds traditional forms of divination useless, so he turns to the "mediums and wizards" whom he had previously banned from the land (1 Sam. 28:3; cf. vv. 4–7). The word *yiddoni*, translated as "wizard," conjuring images of Harry Potter to many modern minds, comes from the Hebrew root *yada* meaning "to know," indicating "one in whom a spirit dwells." Koehler, Baumgartner, and Stamm, *Hebrew and Aramaic Lexicon*, 393.

find the woman from Endor. In Hebrew "Endor" is *ayin dor*, which means "eye of generation." Is she from a place reputed for seeing those who have gone before? As king, Saul has forbidden divination practices, but he disguises himself to seek insight from this medium. At first she refuses to help, fearing for her life, but when Saul offers assurance, she trusts him and conjures Samuel from the dead. Through their exchange, Saul gets the adviser he craves but the prediction he dreads: Samuel announces that the Philistines will defeat Israel and that Saul and his sons will join him—in death—the next day (vv. 15–19).

The aftermath of this sad story is poignant and inspiring (1 Sam. 28:20–25). Terrified, Saul collapses in distress, and the woman of Endor comforts him. She respectfully takes charge of the king. "Look, your maidservant listened to your voice and I put my life in your hands. I listened to your words that you spoke to me. So, you also, now listen to the voice of your maidservant and I will place before you a morsel of bread, then eat, so you will have strength as you go on your way" (vv. 21–22; translation mine). At first Saul refuses, but the woman insists and slaughters a fatted calf to serve the king as his last supper (vv. 24–25).

The only other biblical reference to a fatted calf being served in a milestone meal comes from the Gospel of Luke (15:11–32). Jesus tells the story of the wayward prodigal son who returns home after squandering his fortune. Instead of rejecting or rebuking the selfish son, the young man's father welcomes him home and kills and cooks the fatted calf for a celebratory feast (vv. 22–24). Jesus' scriptures were the Hebrew Scriptures; perhaps he was inspired by a story about the extravagant hospitality of a woman from the town called "eye of generation," who could see departed souls. Like Jesus, another biblical prophet, the medium of Endor combines otherworldly abilities with deep human compassion as she trusts her own spiritual gifts.

As in biblical times, some people today are endowed with prophetic abilities and extraordinary spiritual gifts. One semester, after I gave a lecture on Amos, a student in the class, Kathi, met with me and shared that she also received visions (see Amos 7:7–9; 8:1–3).[12] When I asked for an example, she told me about a Fourth of July celebration when she was with hundreds of others in a park watching a fireworks display. When the horde of people was at its peak, someone started throwing firecrackers into the crowd. Scared and trapped, Kathi silently pleaded in prayer, "Please God—help us!"

"And I got a clear answer," she continued. "God said, 'I am helping you. Look up.'"

As Kathi turned her eyes to the nighttime sky, she saw large angels flying above the crowd with wings that beat back the firecrackers.

"What did the angels look like?" I asked.

"They appeared like people between men and women with long hair and flowing robes and huge wings. I know what I saw," she confided. "And no one was hurt."

Most of us (like me) do not have such wondrous prophetic skills. But we can still pay attention to the spiritual insights that may come to us offering guidance. I attended a yoga retreat once that included a special session on meditation. The instructor urged us to listen to our intuition and asked if anyone had a story they'd like to share. One participant talked about a particular day that started like most others: she was getting ready for work and dressing her toddler to go to daycare. Then a voice inside her head told her that her daughter should not be at the childcare facility that day. "I had to work," the woman explained, "and even though the voice persisted, I did not call my mother or try to make alternate babysitting arrangements." Two hours later, she got a phone call explaining that another child had bitten her daughter. "In the end, my little girl was okay," the participant added, "but I really wish I

---

12. Visions and dreams are a key means of divine-human communication throughout the Bible. For a brief overview, see Niditch, "Prophetic Dreams and Visions."

had listened to that voice." As a result of attending this workshop, when I need to make a decision, I often try to stop and listen for any inner guidance—and I usually find the advice I receive very helpful. I doubt this simple process reflects any prophetic gift, but I think it does hint at vibrant access to spiritual insights that we often ignore or disregard.

I wish the Bible's prophetic legacy for women were simply positive. We recognize prophetic abilities around us and in us and in biblical stories of women prophets. We discover these texts as literary gems, small sparkling narrative nuggets, largely overlooked, that can be picked up, valued (even treasured), and passed along to others who will also appreciate the ways they refract the Bible's light. But prophetic texts can be held up like rot, or worse, to women. Notorious, salacious, malicious interpretations of violent, aggressive, degrading depictions of women can be toxic or even lethal if the dehumanization of women goes unchallenged.

Hosea 1–2 offers one disturbing example.[13] God commands Hosea to take a promiscuous woman as his wife, and he marries Gomer, who bears three children. God instructs Hosea to give their offspring foreboding names: Jezreel (the place of a bloody coup; see 2 Kings 9–10; Hosea 1:4), Lo-ruhamah (meaning "not loved"; Hosea 1:6), and Lo-ammi (meaning "not my people"; 1:9). Hosea then has his two younger children act as his mouthpiece to issue a threatening warning to their mother (!): if Gomer does not stop her unfaithfulness, she will be stripped naked and killed with thirst (2:2–3). Hosea threatens to uncover, shame, and trap his wife so no one will rescue her (vv. 6, 10) until he offers to take her back (vv. 14–20). The prophet proffers portraits of a woman—naked, vulnerable, alone—to shock and shame his audience. Gomer symbolizes Israel's unfaithfulness to Yahweh, as she worships the god Baal. Hosea represents God, who is angry at these idolatrous ways but willing to exonerate her. Biblical commentators often seize on

13. Further examples include Jer. 2–3; 13; and Ezek. 16; 23.

Hosea's forgiveness as a metaphor for God's love. But what about the sadistic, graphic images of an exposed woman and the behavior this chapter silently condones? Cruelty to women is conveyed as acceptable when accompanied by an apology. Such actions of abuse followed by sweet talk fulfill the vile paradigm common in situations of intimate partner violence, here biblically enshrined.

A few years ago, I read a student paper on Hosea 2 that stunned me. Like Hosea and Gomer's children, my student and his brother were trapped in a home of threats that became manifest. Their father would go on rampages, hurting their mother and then, predictably, pledging his undying love to his abused wife (see Hosea 2:2–13, then vv. 14–23). "Forgive and forget, baby." Such pernicious patterns comprise gaslighting, which leads the injured person to question their own experience. "Did this brutality take place? How can he act normal and be sweet and tender after what just happened? Am I remembering the viciousness correctly?" For my student, the situation was dead real. In the end, only he and his brother escaped. His father killed his mother, then himself.

The ways we understand the Bible can have life-or-death consequences. The prophets spoke with such passion because they were trying to save their people from destruction, often from attacking enemies. Pay attention to your emotional reactions to biblical texts. Listen to your own anger, as the prophets do. Prophetic justice soars when people heed warnings and spurn destructive ways. Justice is not always found in the text just as it is; sometimes the reaction from the reading is the real reward.

Perhaps the most valuable way that we profit from prophecy is being led away from harm as individuals and societies. Often prophets in antiquity, like many prophets today, were paid for their services (1 Sam. 9:6–8; 1 Kings 14:1–3; Amos 7:10–13). But for the rest of us, the benefits gained from biblical prophecy are less tangible and more enduring than pecuniary payments. We recognize that prophecy was and still is a widespread phenomenon that draws on the calling and commitment of those who serve as divine-human intermediaries, regardless of gender or age.[14] We appreciate biblical stories of women who are prophets, noting the bravery, skills, insights, and abilities that made them valued as religious, military, political, and spiritual leaders. We are inspired by their witness to take risks in offering courageous compassion. We open our eyes a little wider to look for prophets in our own communities, or even in our own homes. We notice and name our personal spiritual gifts, whatever form they may take, trusting that they strengthen our own connection with the divine. We firmly claim that life and love are God's will for all who live and breathe. We reject harmful interpretations of prophetic texts and embrace readings that promote well-being. And, like anyone who receives a gift, we who study prophecy are grateful for the insights that it makes available to us.

A feminist lens shows prophecy as the purview of all people—including women—and brings us to behold a world that is vibrant with spiritual energy and teeming with passion. Look for the prophets around you, and notice how elements of prophecy may enrich your own life. Hope + faith + courage + justice + words + action + love = worldly and otherworldly profit—see?

---

14. For discussion of children in the Bible, including girls, as prophets, see "Children Can Be Prophets Too" on p. 141 in chapter 10 of this book.

---------- **Questions for Reflection and Conversation** ----------

1. Deborah, Miriam, and Huldah are important religious, political, and spiritual leaders of the Bible. Which women leaders of our time do you admire? Why?

2. Events that defy logic are relatively common in the Bible. What have you witnessed or experienced that did not seem entirely rational? What happened?

3. The woman of Endor goes out of her way to help King Saul when he is troubled and then offers extravagant hospitality when he is deeply distressed. When have you gone out of your way to help someone in a difficult situation, or when has someone done the same for you? When have you offered or received extravagant hospitality? How did you or your relationship with the other person change due to these encounters?

6

The job of Job

I had been sobbing when a student knocked on the door. Seated at my desk, I was holding my head in my hands, face down. If only I could have pretended not to be there, but the door to my office, like all responsible office doors today, had a glass window. I glanced up, and when I saw who was there, I knew this smart, eager learner from my Aramaic class had come to talk with me about Jesus' language. Without feeling like I had much choice, I got up from my desk, opened the door just a little, and offered an explanation for my blotchy crier face.

"My sister just called me. My father is going to die soon."

"My grandpa is dying too!" she instantly exclaimed, rather perkily. Like the two of us were now chums in the same hey-my-loved-one-is-dying club.

My sorrow was replaced by a brief flash of annoyance. I thought, "You're an adult. Don't you expect your grandfather to be dying around now?" In that moment, the irony escaped me. I was a generation older than her; my father and her grandfather were probably not too far from each other in age. What did I expect myself? But these were my father's very last hours of life, and I was so far away.

While my father's health was declining precipitously during his final months, I was teaching a course on Job. That irony had not eluded me. Throughout the semester, I had been standing in front of my students, lecturing on parallel tales from the ancient Near East, the intricacies of Hebrew poetry, and exegetical analyses of texts, while painful, emotional, heartrending aspects of Job's story were unfolding in my own family.

In some ways, my father, David, was like Job. Both men had unwavering faith in God. Job "feared God and turned away from evil" (Job 1:1). My father was a United Methodist minister for fifty-four years who truly believed the messages he preached. Job and my father enjoyed good health. Job's physical state is so strong at the beginning of the book that it doesn't merit mentioning. Like us when our health is fine, we don't need to talk about it. My father exercised regularly before it was a thing and ran the New York City marathon in his sixties. Job has seven sons and three daughters (v. 2). My father also had three daughters (but no sons). Job is ultra-rich (with "seven thousand sheep, three thousand camels, five hundred yoke of oxen, five hundred donkeys, and very many servants"; v. 3). My father definitely was *not* ultra-rich (nary a camel to be found in our parsonage backyard), but he had steady employment his entire adult life, which is its own significant success. Job's sons hold feasts at each other's homes and invite their sisters to eat and drink with them (v. 4). My sisters and I have dinner parties at our homes and invite each other to eat and drink together. Job petitioned God on behalf of his children (v. 5); my father prayed for his children. The text tells us that Job was "blameless and upright" (v. 1) and "the greatest of all the people of the east" (v. 3). My father was a humble person and would never have claimed to be the greatest of all people on the East Coast. Of course, he had his faults, but overall, he was an upright, faithful, caring man. He worked hard for his family and periodically took flak from parishioners for our sakes. This is what he always did (as said of Job, v. 5b).

Unlike my father, Job is set up to appear beyond reproach. The first time he speaks is to explain why he gets up early to make sacrifices on behalf of his children: "It may be that my children have sinned, and cursed God in their hearts" (Job 1:5). Job is so pious and protective of his children that he will cover their potential sins *just in case* they had possibly had an offensive thought. But if you read closely, there is a chink in the paradigmatically perfect armor. Job 1:3 informs us of his "very many servants"; the word for "servants" in this verse, *avudah*, also means "slaves."[1] I remember a student in my Job class, Jeremy, who was raised in Appalachia and refused to accept Job as an admirable, let alone ideal, man, since he owned so many slaves. I couldn't disagree.[2] But for the biblical story to work, we need to first embrace Job as a good guy.

So life goes well for Job, the paragon patriarch, until it does not.

Enter the Lord, who, like important people, chairs meetings. Specifically, the Lord is convening with lesser gods; the Hebrew tells us they are "the sons of the gods" (*bene ha-elohim*; Job 1:6; translation mine). One of these minor deities is *ha-satan*, a word that our Bibles translate as "Satan." Take out that big mental eraser and wipe away the image of a skinny guy in a red suit with pointy ears and an arrow tail, clutching a pitchfork. In its place, imagine a smart guy in a sharply tailored black tunic (just the right amount of tuck at the waist) who left his cosmic office with a wall full of diplomas to take his seat near the front of a long table at this otherworldly assembly. That's *ha-satan* (translated "the adversary"),

---

1. Koehler, Baumgartner, and Stamm, *Hebrew and Aramaic Lexicon*, 777.

2. Slavery in the ancient Near East was very different from slavery in American history, which exploited and tortured people of African descent on a large scale to generate capital, especially from agriculture. In the ancient Near East, most anyone could be made a slave if their land was conquered. Slavery was widespread and slaves became the "alienable, heritable property of the owner." Lewis, "Classical and Near Eastern Slavery in the First Millennium BCE," 6.

the roving prosecutor who trolls the earth looking for those who transgress the way of the Lord (v. 7).

In this meeting, God calls attention to Job as an impeccable model of virtue, but *ha-satan* is not impressed. He points out that to be blameless when you are prosperous is not all that hard. God immediately hands over Job to *ha-satan* to do what he wants with him, except take his health. So *ha-satan* swiftly destroys Job's animals and slaves (i.e., his wealth), children, and family property—but Job remains righteous (Job 1:8–22).

Like Job, my father endured a slew of sudden losses. Toward the end of his life, he and my mother were swindled out of nearly all the money they had saved over the years by a trusted church member (the congregation's treasurer!) who posed as a financial analyst. My parents would get glitzy reports, go to this man's (read: crook's) well-appointed office, and chat amiably with his charming secretary. It was all a show, a staged set, that disappeared one day along with my parents' life savings. This financial devastation happened shortly after my father retired. Just prior, my parents had bought their first home. During all the years of my father's ministry, they had been living in church-owned housing. My mother, Merolyn, his beloved wife of forty-seven years, died suddenly one day of a massive heart attack inside that newly purchased, highly mortgaged house. Her underlying health condition was exacerbated, I am convinced, by the stress of losing all that hard-saved money. Two months after her death, the roof of their house needed repairs, so my father hired a contractor. My dad came to live with my family (about two hours away) while this work was being done. When the contractor working on the roof did not return our calls, we drove to the house to see what was going on. The contractor had ripped off the roof and walked off the job. Rain had poured in, destroying the walls, floors, ceiling, and contents of the roofless house. So, within a short time frame, my father lost wealth, family, and property (with a house falling down [see Job 1:19]), much like Job.

Also like Job, my father still had his health and never wavered in his faith. (And unlike Job, my father did not lose his children.) Job observes that he didn't come into life with anything so why should he leave with anything. "Naked I came from my mother's womb, and naked shall I return there; the LORD gave, and the LORD has taken away; blessed be the name of the LORD" (Job 1:21). Even though Job's possessions and children are gone, he persists in his integrity (2:3). In a second round of ravages, God, rather chillingly, hands over Job to *ha-satan* to attack his health (vv. 4–6). Job's body is covered with "loathsome sores" from head to toe (v. 7). Job sits on an ash heap and scrapes his sores with a piece of broken pottery (v. 8). Once-mighty Job becomes an impoverished portrait of pain.

Job's wife then enters the scene. All she says in the entire book is "Curse God, and die" (Job 2:9), although the Hebrew reads, "Bless God and die." (You might fairly ask, "Excuse me? The translators give the *opposite* of what the text says?" To which I would respond, "Yup."[3]) So instead of readers imagining Job's wife as a supportive partner, we think of her as a blasphemous shrew. Job's response confirms this belittling impression as he insults his wife: "You speak as any foolish woman would speak" (v. 10a).[4] He adds a touch of theological self-righteousness, his voice, I imagine, dripping with condescension: "Shall we receive the good at the hand of God, and not receive the bad?" (v. 10a). Then the narrator chimes in with a further word of patronizing judgment, "In all this Job did not sin with his lips" (v. 10b). You go, Job. Show that woman her place.

I have taught at eight institutions of higher learning over the course of my career; a particular meeting at one of these schools

---

3. For a detailed explanation as to why translators render *barak* ("bless") as "curse" in this verse, see "Job's Wife—Cursing or Blessing?" on p. 144 in chapter 10 of this book.

4. The root of the Hebrew word *nevalot*, rendered as "foolish woman" in this verse (NRSV), carries connotations of being "worthless," "futile," "godless," and "good for nothing." See Koehler, Baumgartner, and Stamm, *Hebrew and Aramaic Lexicon*, 663.

is indelibly memorable. I was relatively new to this faculty and in a department meeting when I voiced an idea. Honestly, I forget the particulars of what I said, but I remember the reaction well. The man who was chairing the meeting said with a smile (and I quote verbatim), "Julie, you ignorant slut."[5] Then he added, to make it all okay, "You know that line comes from old *Saturday Night Live* episodes, right?" My colleagues in the room, all men, chuckled.[6] And, for a second, so did I. That was the pressure: smile and pretend such comments don't matter. But it hit me a few seconds later how easily I had been degraded as a relative newcomer in a professional setting because of my gender. Everyone in the room had colluded, me included. "What if we had just heard a blatantly racist remark instead of a sexist one," I thought. "Would we all have laughed and moved on?"

After the meeting, I confronted the person who made this comment, and he genuinely apologized. I forgave him and told him that I have also said things I have regretted and been sorry afterward. I then asked to give a PowerPoint presentation at a subsequent department meeting on the impact of language, which I did. In this presentation, I incorporated linguistic theory from Edward Sapir and Benjamin Whorf.[7] I included a film clip of the "ignorant slut" bit from *Saturday Night Live* and deconstructed the scene using feminist analysis. I realize that creating this presentation was not my work to do. It would have been much better for the person who made the remark to address our colleagues, but he did not offer, and I wanted the room to recognize what had happened, so took on the job myself. This colleague and I were able

5. Please do not ask me the name of this person or where this meeting took place. I will not tell you.

6. Two of my male colleagues privately apologized to me later for not saying anything in that moment. There was one other woman who usually attended these meetings, but she was not present that day.

7. Edward Sapir and his student at Yale, Benjamin Whorf, were among the first to explore the relationship between language and behavior. See Carroll, *Language, Thought, and Reality*, 134–37.

to work through this incident and remain on good terms. Yet it hurt to be demeaned. Job's wife and I are both wives and women. Aside from that, we do not have a lot in common, except that we can both be put down by insults directly related to being female.

Both scenes of interaction (Job's wife speaking and my faculty meeting) reveal the potential power of those around you. What happens when you are in a tough spot? Do people show up for you? Do they say anything? Do they somehow advocate or intervene? What do you and I do when we witness someone else being treated unfairly? Job's wife, the only woman who speaks in this biblical book, is on her own. Her husband puts her down, and she is bereft of friends. But Job, the once-powerful patriarch who now sits shriveled on an ash heap, does have friends. And they come to him in his distress.

When I was a pastor of a congregation, parishioners used to ask me what to say or do when someone they knew was suffering. Their loved one just got diagnosed with cancer, for instance, and they didn't want to offer cheery, hollow platitudes or enter into conversations about what might really happen. Taking my Bible, I would turn to Job at the end of chapter two. "Look at what Job's friends do when he is in anguish," I would point out. "Just show up."

Job's friends—Eliphaz, Bildad, and Zophar—start out embodying solidarity with devastated Job. At first glance, they do not even recognize him without his health or the trappings of his once-opulent life. Upon realizing that this withered human was their once-admired friend, they weep, rend their garments, and throw dust on their own heads (Job 2:11–12). Then Eliphaz, Bildad, and Zophar provide what is known in pastoral care as a "non-anxious presence": "They sat with him on the ground seven days and seven nights, and no one spoke a word to him, for they saw that his suffering was very great" (v. 13). Job's friends show up.

Job and his friends then engage in a series of poetic dialogues in which his friends give advice and Job responds. When my parents lost all their money, I also had friends who volunteered commentary. "Oh well, too bad," said one friend, with a literal shrug of his shoulder when I shared what had happened to their finances. He moved on rather quickly from pondering my parents' new situation; it didn't affect him. Another friend was gentler in her approach. "Some things are better not to think about," she suggested kindly. She was right; what good would it do to dwell on this loss? After sitting with Job silently for seven days, Job's friends try a different tack. They open their mouths, and their value as friends plummets. Job's friends spend the next thirty-four chapters telling Job why he must have deserved his lamentable fate.

Eliphaz, Bildad, and Zophar are stuck in the traditional worldview of wisdom. Wisdom books in the Bible focus on the individual and offer counsel and insight on how to live one's life.[8] In Proverbs, the universe is cause and effect: do good, you are rewarded; do bad, you are punished. The book of Job turns this idea on its head and asks, "Really?!" by showing a virtuous person who endures undeserved strife. Job's friends are convinced that he must have done something terribly wrong—otherwise why would this calamity have befallen him? They cling to a cause-and-effect way of understanding the universe because it works for them. They are safe and believe that Job's actions must have led to his misery. This theology—that horrible things happen to those who deserve the trouble—is as common ("it must be God's will") as it is cruel (blaming the sufferer for their pain).

The books of Proverbs and Job offer opposing worldviews. As often happens in the Bible, insights do not come from only one source but can be gleaned from different books or chapters or passages—including when views are in tension with each other. We listen to the dialogue or even argument between two perspectives, as with Job and his friends, and try to tease out whatever truths

8. The Wisdom books of the Bible are Job, Proverbs, and Ecclesiastes, plus certain Psalms that are categorized as wisdom psalms.

arise from the interplay of voices. The astute Bible reader acts as the book's marriage counselor. The goal is not to try to force two perspectives to be the same but, rather, to seek understanding. We must recognize that truths vary according to perspective. Our paradoxical goal as readers is to be both critical (whose interests are served here?) and open-minded (let me genuinely listen).

Job's friends do not genuinely listen to him. Eliphaz is the first to speak and tells Job to stop being so impatient (Job 4:5). He has a point. While people commonly refer to "the patience of Job," beyond chapter two, patient Job is replaced by upset, angry, frustrated, bitter Job. Job must have sinned, Eliphaz reasons: "Who that was innocent ever perished?" (4:7). (Um . . . lots of people.) Eliphaz further instructs Job to be more pious: "As for me, I would seek God, and to God I would commit my cause. He does great things and unsearchable, marvelous things without number" (5:8–9).

The second friend to speak, Bildad, also clings to the conviction that God is just, so therefore Job must be guilty of shameful acts. "Does God pervert justice? Or does the Almighty pervert the right?" (Job 8:3). In an insult-to-injury rhetorical move, Bildad even implies that Job's destroyed children got what they deserved: "If your children sinned against him, he delivered them into the power of their transgression" (v. 4). Also a fixer, Bildad sanctimoniously proposes a solution: "If you will seek God and make supplication to the Almighty, if you are pure and upright, surely then he will rouse himself for you and restore to you your rightful place" (vv. 5–6). After each friend speaks, Job responds, pouring out his anguish and defending himself.

Zophar, the third friend to show up, appears fed up with this back and forth. He essentially tells Job that, despite his current tortured state, he probably got off easy: "Know then that God exacts of you less than your guilt deserves" (Job 11:6b). Who are you to know the mind of God, Job? Ironically, of course, the friends accuse Job of doing what they do themselves, and what so many of us do: hold on to bad theology. Bad (and by "bad" I mean "harmful") theology can saturate our thinking.

My cousin's daughter died when she was eleven years old. Meghan had freckles and long red hair. She loved reading, writing stories, and playing the flute in her school band. She and I were both the oldest of three daughters; the six of us formed "the sisters club." I remember one evening at my grandmother's house when both sets of daughters were dancing to the Bangles song "Walk Like an Egyptian." We strutted around the living room making profile poses, elbows and wrists at sharp right angles, while singing and laughing at ourselves. About a year later, Meghan needed to get her tonsils out. No problem, right? But she had a massive pulmonary embolism. After the operation, a blood clot formed in one of her legs, traveled to her lungs while she slept, and cut off all air. She came home from the hospital and, with no warning, was dead the next day.

Compounding this tragedy were the theological platitudes that well-intentioned friends dropped like daggers: "I'll never understand the will of God," and "I guess God needed another angel." If someone finds it comforting to believe that God took a child because God needed that specific angel so badly, then I guess that is okay for them. But who would want to worship a god like that? A god who plays with people's lives and inflicts pain out of self-serving desires. A god who is selfish and spiteful. No thanks, not me. And not Job either.

After a series of dialogues with the friends, plus a fourth younger friend, Elihu, who pipes in mostly with more of the same blame-the-victim game (Job 32–37), God finally speaks up (Job 38). Job has been responding to his friends, arguing with their reasoning. His speeches also appeal to God, pleading for intervention. But when God finally emerges to answer Job, it is not the God that Job expects. Instead of a kindly patriarch who explains the wager that (oh yeah) destroyed Job's life, or maybe even apologizes, we meet a God who poetically bellows, in essence, "I'm God, and you're not." Job has been calling God to account, and God pushes back. From the destabilizing gales of a whirlwind, God even bullies Job: "Gird up your loins like a man, I will question you, and you shall declare to me" (v. 3). You want a debate, Job? You're on. Against me. *The Creator of the World*. Good luck.

Job has been begging God for understanding of all that has befallen him and pleading for mercy in his misery, but he gets a zoo tour. After reviewing the wonders of the cosmos that God made and Job most definitely did not, God describes the habits of animals: the hunting lions, the mountain goats giving birth, the donkey running on the steppes, the ox laboring for humans, the ostrich flapping her wings, the horse leaping like a locust, and the hawk making its nest (Job 38:39–39:30). God is telling Job, in effect, "I made the world and all its creatures, Job. Who do you think *you* are to complain to *me*?!" Job meekly responds only to say that he will be quiet, but God is not done and challenges Job again (40:1–9). This time, God points out marvelous, mystical beasts: the Behemoth and the Leviathan, with their awe-inspiring strength (40:15–41:34). What can Job say? What can he do, except acknowledge God's greatness?

Job's final speech reveals theological truth. "I have uttered what I did not understand," Job admits (42:3). He was clinging, like so many of us do, to a bad (and by "bad" I mean "harmful") conception of God. He thought God was a powerful man, like him.[9] This idea of God is surprisingly close to the surface for many of us because of the powerful men who (pretty much) wrote the Bible and the powerful men who (pretty much) interpret it. Their idea of God justifies their own power. But how dare we, like Job, limit God? Even God is angry at being boxed in. This is not the lord of kingdoms, corporations, or creeds but rather the God of creation, creatures, and cosmos.

9. For further discussion of models of God in Job, see Newsom, "Job," 214–15. See also her more extensive treatment of "the voice from the whirlwind" in *Book of Job*, 234–58.

In Hebrew, Job's last words are very different from what we read in English. The NRSV Bible has Job saying, "Therefore I despise myself, and repent in dust and ashes" (42:6). But the Hebrew of Job 42:6 more closely reads, "Therefore I reject and console myself, upon dust and ashes." The Hebrew does not have Job hating himself, just rejecting. But rejecting what? Job is still on the ash heap, where he has been for forty chapters, an incarnation of abject humility. Perhaps he learns what he needs to discover—that God is not a patriarch like him—and he rejects his earlier conception of God. Job finds comfort in shedding this damaging, entrenched theology. And that realization is profoundly feminist.

Like a feminist, Job holds on to the truth of his own story. He does not agree with his friends that his suffering was somehow deserved. It was not God's will that my parents had their life savings stolen or that Meghan died at age eleven. I did not deserve to be called a slut in a department meeting. Hold on to the truth of your own story. Interpret it as you choose, not as others want you to in order to serve their agendas. Job tenaciously clings to what he knows to be true and is rewarded for it in the end.

Once Job rejects toxic theology, God affirms his views and rebukes his friends. Speaking to Eliphaz, God twice asserts, "You have not spoken of me what is right, as my servant Job has" (42:7, 8). The friends must offer up burnt offerings, setting ablaze bulls and rams as an extravagant sacrifice to seek God's favor (v. 8). Job intercedes for them, "and the LORD accepted Job's prayer" and "restored the fortunes of Job" (vv. 9–10).

In the end, Job gets nearly everything back and then some. His brothers and sisters and "all who had known him before" come and eat with him, sharing sympathy and comfort. They give Job gifts: pieces of money and a gold ring (42:11). Not to be outdone, the Lord then bestows upon Job twice as many animals as he had had before losing everything (fourteen thousand sheep, six thousand camels, one thousand yoke of oxen, and one thousand donkeys (v. 12; cf. 1:3)! He gets a brand-new family with another seven sons and three daughters. To us, the replacement family feels like an affront. What about the former children; don't they count? But the narrator here just wants to make a clear point: Job has his children and lots of riches. The only thing that is not restored to Job is slaves (1:3; cf. 42:12).[10] It seems that Job has gained empathy regarding the abuse of others as the lessons from his ash-heap experience run deep. And Job still has the courage and strength to go on. Restoration is possible, even for the most tormented sufferer. Job is back to his former, glorious self.

Except he is not.

Like a budding feminist, Job has gained critical knowledge regarding women and girls. They matter just as much as men and boys. To emphasize this point, the end of Job's story shows his daughters as even more important than his sons. Job's final actions are to name his daughters and ensure their inheritance. While the sons remain anonymous, Job gives his daughters auspicious names (42:14). The first is named Jemimah, meaning "dove": may this girl have freedom. The second is Keziah, meaning "cinnamon flowers": may this girl know the subtle sweetness of life.[11] The third is Keren-happuch, meaning "horn of antimony." A horn could be used as a container, and antimony is a mineral that was ground into a paste as a cosmetic. So perhaps Job is naming his youngest daughter after a beauty treatment, but horns were also an ancient Near Eastern symbol of power, and antimony is always combined with another compound.[12] Perhaps Job is imparting strength and solidarity to Keren-happuch.

Further indicating his appreciation of the rights of women and girls, Job gives his daughters an inheritance along with the sons

---

10. I am grateful to Neal Medlyn for this insight.

11. A second definition for "Keziah" signifies a bow (weapon). Perhaps Job wants his daughter to be able to protect herself. See Koehler, Baumgartner, and Stamm, *Hebrew and Aramaic Lexicon*, 1122.

12. The Hebrew word *happuch* conveys the mineral called "antimony" from the Greek *anti-monos* meaning "not alone."

(42:15). To bequeath property and belongings to girls was almost unheard of in the biblical world. Nowhere else in the Bible do we read of girls inheriting along with their brothers.[13] Yet better than anyone else in the entire Bible, Job knows how hard life can suddenly become. True to feminist ideals, he is dedicated to ensuring his daughters' success. We infer that his daughters thrived and continued his family, as the text goes on to affirm that Job "saw his children, and his children's children, four generations. And Job died, old and full of days" (42:16–17).

Job shares feminist wisdom, as his bestowal extends not only to his children but also to us as readers. The job of Job is not to be patient (he isn't) or to silently endure abuse (he doesn't). Rather, Job's job is to challenge oppressive understandings of God. This male-centered biblical book is surprisingly full of feminist insight: Trust the integrity of your own words. Speak your truth, even when others would prefer you stay silent. Job, in essence, teaches us how to be good feminists.

My father did the same with his three daughters. I write this now with tears in my eyes, grateful for both my father and my mother, who believed in my sisters and me, and missing them. They were not perfect. (You show me someone with a perfect life, and I'll show you someone you don't know too well.) But they were loving parents who bequeathed to their daughters a conviction that the book of Job also passes on to you: believe in your own voice and the power of your story.

13. Numbers 27:1–8 shows the daughters of Zelophehad inheriting property but only because they had no brothers.

────────── **Questions for Reflection and Conversation** ──────────

1. Job has a reputation for being patient, even though he is not patient throughout most of this biblical book. What is your reputation? With whom? Do you think this impression that others have of you is accurate? Why or why not?

2. When Job's friends come to be with him in his distress, they are silent at first, and then they offer lots of advice. What advice have you received that you remember? Was it helpful?

3. At the end of the book, Job gives his daughters names with meanings that carry blessings. What does your name mean? How did you get your name? Do you think your name fits you well? Why or why not?

Guns and Psalms

In a song from the musical *Rent*, the lead character asks why years of his life are entirely forgotten when scenes from one magic night "forever flicker in close-up on the 3-D IMAX of my mind?" That line poses a profound question with a surprisingly simple answer: emotions. While most moments fade into an irretrievable ether, some are seared into our brains because of the intensity of our feelings. Emotions matter in our gray matter. The book of Psalms revels in this truth, conveying happiness, anger, gratitude, fear, and trust.

The collection of poems that forms Psalms is unique. This biblical book has more chapters than any other—150—each an individual psalm.[1] Like the Torah, Psalms is divided into five different books.[2] The compilation of Psalms can be excerpted from the rest of the Bible for use as a devotional resource (the Psalter), and it plays a central role in the life of faith communities. The song-poems of Psalms are grounded in the divine-human connection. Praises and

---

1. The shortest is Ps. 117, with just two verses, and the longest is Ps. 119 with 176 verses.

2. These divisions are marked within the text by a concluding line, usually of benediction, signaling the end of a collection (books 1–5 consist of Pss. 1–41; 42–72; 73–89; 90–106; and 107–50, respectively).

pleas voicing joys and needs go directly to God, who is not too busy frying bigger fish but cares about each puny human minnow. This conviction prompts intimate sharing from the psalmist, the person whose voice we hear in a particular psalm. Yet God remains steadfastly silent, which is also unusual. If you know the Hebrew words *vayomer Adonai*, translated as "the Lord said," you have learned 4 percent of the Old Testament in its original language. God can be chatty in the Hebrew Bible but not in the book of Psalms.

In the Bible, all poetry is presented as speech—someone is saying these words.[3] Like music, these poems are an outpouring of the soul. Compact language juxtaposes phrases in episodic bursts of meaning. We cannot skim a poem and expect much benefit from our reading. Instead, poems invite us to pause and ponder. The space offered by the poetic page offers room to wend one's way into the images. A poem can be enigmatic and elusive, perhaps like God.

Poetry in the Hebrew Bible is characterized by the interplay in a set of poetic lines, usually two (a couplet) but sometimes three (a tercet). Robert Lowth, an Anglican bishop in eighteenth-century England, called this feature "parallelism." He identified three major patterns: synonymous parallelism, in which the second line agrees with the first; antithetic parallelism, in which the second line contrasts the first; and synthetic parallelism, in which the lines relate to each other without agreement or disagreement (i.e., the miscellaneous category). Subsequent scholars have questioned and refined Lowth's schema.[4]

As a simplified modern analogy, I suggest that the second line in parallelism can be loosely compared to an ancient emoji. What comes after a segment of text helps you interpret what you have

---

3. While all poetry in the Hebrew Bible is speech, not all speech is poetry (narratives contain dialogue that is not in poetic form). When you see poetry in your Bible (laid out on the page with lots of white space), you are reading words placed in someone's mouth. The speaker can be anonymous (like a person offering psalms to God) or well known (like the prophets with books named after them).

4. For an overview of parallelism, see Creach, *Discovering Psalms*, 33–41.

just read. For example, the beloved Psalm 23 begins: "The LORD is my shepherd." How should we understand this assertion? The Lord is my shepherd / so I am a dirty sheep(?). The Lord is my shepherd / who hits me with a staff(?). The Lord is my shepherd / whom I will follow blindly(?). The second line explains: "I shall not want." The Lord is my shepherd / so I lack nothing. Some emojis can fulfill a similar function:

The Lord is my shepherd / 👍.

The Lord is my shepherd / so I'm good. Like an emoji, the second line of a couplet brings interpretation or explanation, setting the tone and providing meaning.[5]

Along with the evocative power of poetry, psalms grip the soul with music. Many psalms were probably sung; the word "psalms" comes from the Greek *psalmos* which means "to sing to the accompaniment of the harp or lyre." Vibrations from inside our bodies resonate with the instruments that humans create to amplify emotional expression.

Early in Genesis, just after the world has been formed with its heavenly stellar bodies and earthly messy ones, music is born: "Lamech took two wives; the name of the one was Adah, and the name of the other Zillah. Adah bore Jabal; he was the ancestor of those who live in tents and have livestock. His brother's name was Jubal; he was the ancestor of all those who play the lyre and pipe. Zillah bore Tubal-cain, who made all kinds of bronze and iron tools. The sister of Tubal-cain was Naamah" (4:19–22).

Notice the children of Lamech and his wives, Adah and Zillah. First comes Jabal, bringer of shelter and keeper of livestock; next, Jubal, ancestor of instrumental sound; and third—*after*

---

5. Zechariah 9:9b offers an example of synonymous parallelism in describing how the king will enter Zion: "humble and riding on a donkey / [then repeating] on a colt, the foal of a donkey." Quoting Zechariah but not understanding parallelism, Matthew's Gospel portrays Jesus as riding into Jerusalem on two animals (not easy!) to fulfill the Scriptures (Matt. 21:1–7).

music—Tubal-cain, maker of tools. Naamah is the half-sister of Jabal and Jubal and the full sister of Tubal-cain; all siblings appear to have a foundational role in establishing human culture. While Naamah's vocation is not explicitly stated, Carol Meyers suggests that she may be the founder of vocal music, since her name comes from the root word *naam* meaning "to be pleasant" or "to sing."[6] Different kinds of people—including parents and siblings—have a role in providing essential elements of civilization, including music. At the outset, the Bible offers room for lyrical feelings that reach their biblical crescendo in the Psalms.

Perhaps the most famous musician in the Bible is David, who traditionally has been credited with writing the Psalms. The close association between David and the Psalter extends back to antiquity, although scholars question this blanket authorial assumption. Once a shepherd and lyre player (1 Sam. 16), David rose to rule Israel when the realm was at its zenith. Nearly half of the psalms include the Hebrew words *le-David* in the first line, rendered "a Psalm of David," although the preposition *le* is most commonly translated "to, for, in regards to"[7] or "to, towards" and as an expression of purpose.[8] But some of the psalms, including those with *le-David* headings, refer to circumstances after David's lifetime.[9] Presuming that David wrote these psalms can lead to problematic interpretations.

Recently I heard a sermon on David and Psalm 51. As the preacher noted, the first line creates the context for what follows: "To the leader. A Psalm of David, when the prophet Nathan came to him,

---

6. Meyers, "Naamah 1," 129. See also Brown, Driver, and Briggs, *Hebrew and English Lexicon*, 654; Koehler, Baumgartner, and Stamm, *Hebrew and Aramaic Lexicon*, 705.

7. Brown, Driver, and Briggs, *Hebrew and English Lexicon*, 510.

8. Koehler, Baumgartner, and Stamm, *Hebrew and Aramaic Lexicon*, 508.

9. For example, references to the Jerusalem temple appear in *le-David* Psalms, but the temple was not built until after David's death (see Ps. 5:7 [MT 5:8]; 11:4; 18:6 [MT 18:7]; 27:4; 29:9; 30:0 [MT 30:1]; 65:4 [MT 65:5]; 68:29 [MT 68:30]; 138:2; cf. 1 Kings 2:10; 6:1).

after he had gone in to Bathsheba." Wearing his doctoral preaching gown and towering above the congregation in an ornately carved limestone pulpit, the minister extolled David's humility. "The greatest king of Israel—the warrior, musician, husband, father, and ruler—pours out his heart in sorrow seeking forgiveness from God. As should we." I sat politely in the pew, feeling anything but inspired. After the introductory line (or superscription), Psalm 51 does not make a single reference to King David.[10] And while this psalmist is full of abject contrition, narratives in 2 Samuel and 1 Kings show David as full of selfish ambition. He commits adultery with Bathsheba then makes sure that her husband, Uriah, dies in battle (2 Sam. 11). When his own son, Amnon, rapes his daughter (and Amnon's half-sister), Tamar, David does nothing to help or defend her (13:1–21). On his deathbed, like a godfather don, David commands his son Solomon to fulfill his murderous wishes (1 Kings 2:5–9). So there's that. "Of course, David was not perfect," the preacher continued, glossing over chapters of ruthlessness in one clause, "but see how he confesses before God: 'Against you, you alone, have I sinned'" (Ps. 51:4). "Against you *alone*?" I thought. Really? Not Bathsheba? Not Uriah? Not Tamar? Not everyone else David dispatched? Confessing to God is a whole lot easier than facing someone whom we have wronged, sincerely apologizing, and actively working to make amends. When we identify Psalm 51 as words of David, we are pulled in by the psalm's remorseful tone. But we need to be wary of easily dismissing David's mistreatment of others; such reasoning might enable us to minimize harm we inflict ourselves.

Even though David did not author the whole book of Psalms, there are nonetheless theological and emotional points of contact between stories about him and select psalms. But if we associate

---

10. Indeed, Ps. 51 urges rebuilding the walls of Jerusalem (v. 18; MT 51:20), which had not yet been destroyed in the time of David.

the Psalms with David too closely, we link these poems to one man, making them misleadingly androcentric.

Women also offer psalms in the Bible. In Exodus 15, right after the Israelites have escaped from slavery and crossed the Red Sea, Miriam, the sister of Moses, embodies the joy of freedom. Taking a hand drum, she leads the Israelite women in singing and dancing while offering a psalm of praise to the Lord for tossing the Egyptian horses and riders into the sea (15:20–21).[11] In Judges 5, Deborah, the prophet and military commander, sings a psalm extolling the Lord as the divine warrior who causes the earth to tremble, the heavens to shower, and the mountains to quake (vv. 3–5). In 1 Samuel 2, Hannah, the mother of the priest Samuel, expresses happiness in a psalm of praise, audaciously declaring a theology of radical reversals, even as she herself, once barren, has borne a child (vv. 4–8). Centuries later, Mary, the mother of Jesus (who is named after Miriam), offers a psalm of gratitude modeled after Hannah's.

Hannah prayed and said,

> "My heart exults in the LORD;
> my strength is exalted in my God." (1 Sam. 2:1a)

And Mary [Greek: *Mariam*] said,

> "My soul magnifies the Lord,
> and my spirit rejoices in God my Savior." (Luke 1:46–47)

Compare the words of these women with those found in the book of Psalms:

> The LORD is my strength and my shield;
> in him my heart trusts;

11. For further discussion of hand drums and women as makers of music in antiquity, see "Women Musicians in the Ancient Near East" on p. 147 in chapter 10 of this book.

so I am helped, and my heart exults,
    and with my song I give thanks to him. (28:7)

I will praise the name of God with a song;
    I will magnify him with thanksgiving. (69:30; MT 69:31)[12]

Phrases from Deborah's and Miriam's psalms are also reflected within the book of Psalms.[13] Deborah's song in Judges 5 may be the oldest literary fragment in the Bible, dating back to the late second millennium BCE (or a little over one thousand years before Jesus was born). Mary's song in Luke's Gospel dates to the latter part of the first century CE (after Jesus was born).[14] This range, with the book of Psalms nestled chronologically and textually in between, shows a long and strong tradition of women as pray-ers and singers of psalms. Beyond David, psalms belong on the lips of all people who feel faith in their bones.

Scholars place the psalms into different genres or types, loosely linked to emotions or themes, and call this approach "form criticism."[15] Think of modern pop songs that can be grouped into categories, like the "I love you, you're perfect" or the "I adore you and will never have you" or the "you're gone and I'm fine" songs. Each type of song generally follows a predictable pattern (e.g.,

12. The abbreviation MT stands for "Masoretic Text" and refers to the Hebrew text with vowel markings added by Jewish scribes (known as Masoretes) in the fifth to tenth centuries CE. In some parts of the Bible, notably Psalms, verse numbers are slightly different in Hebrew and English Bibles.

13. In Judg. 5:3b, Deborah declares, "I will sing, I will make melody to the LORD, the God of Israel," similar to Ps. 108:1b (MT 108:2b): "I will sing and make melody. Awake, my soul!" Miriam's song in Exod. 15:21, "Sing to the LORD, for he has triumphed gloriously" resonates with Ps. 98:1: "O sing to the LORD a new song, for he has done marvelous things."

14. I use the abbreviations BCE meaning "Before Common Era" (instead of BC meaning "Before Christ") and CE meaning "Common Era" (instead of "AD" meaning *Anno Domini* or the "year of our Lord"). The abbreviations BCE and CE are nonconfessional ways of referring to the same chronological divisions.

15. German scholar Hermann Gunkel (1862–1932) introduced form criticism as a way of analyzing biblical texts and developed this approach in his commentary on the Psalms (Gunkel, *Introduction to Psalms*).

you left, it was hard, now I'm better off; like Gloria Gaynor's "I Will Survive"). Psalms are similar. Just as a song does not state, "This is a 'good riddance' song," the genre is not named, but it can be deduced by those who hear or read the psalm. Classifications are therefore somewhat fluid. Lament psalms mourn a situation and seek God's intervention; praise psalms offer thanks from an individual or community; and royal psalms celebrate God as the heavenly king.[16] The title of a book by the writer Anne Lamott, *Help, Thanks, Wow*, essentially sums up the three main types of psalms. Perhaps not surprisingly, the most prevalent psalms are those that cry for help.

In Hebrew, many of these lament psalms include the word *lamah*, or "why?" The similarity in sound offers a mnemonic aid: *lamah/lam*ent. The worried, scared psalmist interrogates God: "Why, O Lord, do you stand far off?" (Ps. 10:1); "Why have you forsaken me?" (22:1; MT 22:2); "Why do you hide your face? Why do you forget our affliction and oppression?" (44:24; MT 44:25). We also ask these questions: I'm a good person; why did this awful thing happen to me? Why did this relationship that I cherished fall apart? Why did this person whom I love die? Why did I lose my job? my health? my home? my happiness? Why, God? You are supposed to be all-powerful. I believed in you. I trusted you. What good did it do me? Why didn't you prevent or restore this horrible situation?

Like us, the ancient psalmists know that life is fragile; everything can change in an instant. Waves of disappointment, betrayal, loss, fear, loneliness, grief, hurt, sickness, sorrow, and even terror can make our life journeys unsteady. Sometimes these waves come crashing over us, threatening our very existence. Why doesn't God just make things right?

I do not believe that God's power is a silver bullet that blows away the difficulties or destroys the pain or evil in our lives with

---

16. Other genres (including subgenres) include Pilgrimage, Trust, Wisdom, Torah, Liturgy, Creation, History, Zion, and Enthronement psalms. See Creach, *Discovering Psalms*, 63–79.

one shot. Rather, the power of God is the power of love. I believe that God is always present loving us, but sometimes we have a hard time recognizing that love. When we suffer, knowing that we are loved can make all the difference between getting to the other side of the situation . . . or not.

Psalms are brave. They dare to traffic in extremes of emotions, even those that scare us most. Depression, for example, can be terrifying. I fear what depression can do to a person because my daughter, Mari, has bipolar II disorder. Unlike bipolar I, in which a person alternates between prolonged periods of mania (heightened energy and potential reckless behavior) and shorter spans of depression (lack of energy and potential feelings of worthlessness), those diagnosed with bipolar II experience longer periods of depression and shorter episodes of a less intense mania (hypomania). This neurological condition can be fatal as it may lead people to take their own lives.

Into the dismal pits of despair, psalmists accompany the suffering soul:

> Turn, O LORD, save my life;
>> deliver me for the sake of your steadfast love.
>>> (6:4; MT 6:5)

> I am weary with my moaning;
>> every night I flood my bed with tears;
>> I drench my couch with my weeping. (6:6; MT 6:7)

> Consider and answer me, O LORD my God!
>> Give light to my eyes, or I will sleep the sleep of death.
>>> (13:3; MT 13:4)

The psalmist fears irrecoverable sinking in the slow quicksand of sorrow. And yet the psalms are grounded in hope through relationship with God. The invisible, mystical, wondrous rope that the psalmist grasps to help pull herself up is faith. Faith also helps Mari deal with her depression, along with the crucial components of medication and therapy. And humor.

Mari talks candidly about her bipolar condition in the standup routine that she performs in New York City comedy clubs. Picture a large, dark room filled with people sitting in clusters of chairs around small tables, bar prominently on one side, the light centered on a raised platform with a standing microphone. I am at one of the tables with my husband and a few friends, in front of me a glistening margarita (lime, on the rocks, salt rim) on a slightly soaked coaster. After a few comedians have shared their routines ("My name is Kimberly, and I'm forty- . . . nine. But it's pronounced 'forty'—the nine is silent"[17]), Mari takes the stage.

"Hi, I'm Mari. I'm five foot four, I live in Brooklyn, and I have bipolar disorder." She picks out someone in the crowd. "You look like you don't believe me. . . . I *am* five foot four. . . . When my psychiatrist told me my diagnosis, she said, 'You have bipolar disorder, it's chronic, potentially lethal, and, just to reiterate, "chronic" means it will never go away.' Talk about ripping off a Band-Aid!"

I hear the laughter and see some expressions of surprise as my daughter risks being vulnerable to break down stigmas against mental illness.[18] Mari on the stage and the Psalms on the page caringly carry the torment of the soul to the reading light or the spotlight. Warmth and energy elbow in to murky, constricted, inner places, breaking up gloom with hopeful spaces.

But Psalms can also be tough. Some psalms are so full of vitriol that religious communities entirely ignore them or edit them

---

17. Kimberly Oser performing at the West Side Comedy Club in Manhattan on February 5, 2022.

18. Along with a friend, Taha Rakla, who has bipolar I, Mari hosts a podcast (*Beautiful Bipolar Badass*) that talks with honesty and levity about bipolar disorder (Crawford and Rakla, "One Flew over the Cuckoo's Nest," and "What Is Bipolar Disorder," available on Spotify).

for worship.[19] Psalm 137, for example, conveys a wistful image of Judean captives. Far from her homeland, exiled to the land of the Euphrates and Tigris (the rivers of Babylon), the psalmist sits under willow trees (although the Hebrew suggests "poplars") and sadly hangs up her lyre, unable to sing as she mourns, missing Jerusalem.[20] The musical *Godspell* popularized this psalm in the song "On the Willows." High notes voice the plaintive plea, "How can we sing? Sing the Lord's songs? In a foreign land?" While the song ends after verse 4, the psalm continues, its tenor descending as the psalmist asks to be physically maimed if she forgets Jerusalem (vv. 5–6). Liturgical readings of Psalm 137 stop there. Still the psalm goes on, first seeking vengeance on the Edomites who urged Jerusalem's fall, and then on the conqueror Babylon (vv. 7–8). The final verse blesses the bashers of baby Babylonians: "Happy are those who grasp and smash your infants against the rock!" (v. 9; translation mine). What do we do with such violent psalms?[21]

Commentators offer a few suggestions. God is the champion of the underdogs, raising them up while bringing enemies down. These songs are cries for justice; those who harm others must suffer the consequences. Vengeance psalms provide a safety valve against violence: the psalmist does not act out of hatred but leaves the revenge to God. But don't violent words abet violent actions? Brutal psalms can be dangerous.

Also concerning are the psalms that hurt women. Hands down, my least favorite psalm is Psalm 45. Classified as a royal psalm, Psalm 45 begins with lavish praise of a handsome, gracious, forever-blessed king (vv. 1–2).[22] Sexual innuendos swiftly arise

19. Fifty-one of the 150 Psalms are not included in the schedule of weekly Christian Bible readings adopted by Protestant and Catholic traditions (called the Revised Common Lectionary). For the full list of omitted Psalms, see Van Harn and Strawn, *Psalms for Preaching and Worship*, 34n79.

20. For the translation of *aravim* as "poplars," see Brown, Driver, and Briggs, *Hebrew and English Lexicon*, 788. For discussion of women as psalmists, see Knowles, "Feminist Interpretation of the Psalms," 427–32.

21. See also Pss. 33; 58; 69; 94; 109; 139.

22. Versification here follows the English (MT verse numbers are one higher).

with references to the "sword on [his] thigh" (v. 3), extolling his majesty (v. 4) with his sharp arrows (v. 5), and his upright scepter (v. 6). This breathtaking man is anointed by God (v. 7) and resides in an ivory palace (v. 8). The over-the-top encomium goes on to describe his harem (v. 9). Whereas the NRSV portrays daughters of kings "among your ladies of honor," the Hebrew calls these princesses "your precious ones" (*yiqqrotekha*; v. 9). At the king's right hand is the "queen" (Hebrew: *shegal*), decked in gold. This unusual term for "queen" (typically *malkah*) sounds close to the word *shagel*, which means "to violate."[23] One of the king's women is told to obey, look, and listen: "Forget your people and your father's house" (v. 10). The next verse describes her purpose and role: the king will crave her beauty; he is her lord, and she should prostrate herself before him (v. 11). The Hebrew is tricky in verses 12–13 but seems to show daughters of Tyre carrying gifts to the princess, who wears a gold robe (v. 14). Along with more young women, she is brought to the royal residence of the king (v. 15). He is promised male progeny, who will become princes (v. 16), and generations will shower him with eternal praise (v. 17). Psalm 45 offers a common male fantasy (riches! power! limitless, beautiful, adoring women!) that has become enshrined in religious tradition.[24] But images of subjugation invite interrogation. When over a third of the Psalms are deemed inappropriate for the weekly church readings, why do we continue to read this psalm in congregations, when it promotes such toxic ideas of vaulted male supremacy and objectifying female subservience? When the rest of the congregation recites Psalm 45 aloud in worship, I remain silent as a sphinx.

While Psalm 45 is my least-liked psalm, Psalm 121 is my favorite. This Psalm and I share a memory from one day, decades ago,

---

23. See Brown, Driver, and Briggs, *Hebrew and English Lexicon*, 993, which denies an etymological (derivative) association, although a paronomastic (sound) connection remains.

24. Psalm 45 is read twice in the cycle of the Revised Common Lectionary and three times in the cycle of the Episcopal lectionary.

that forever flickers in close-up on the 3-D IMAX of my mind. While in seminary, I spent a semester in Central America studying liberation theology.[25] This particular day I was in Nicaragua and hitchhiking from Estelí to a small northern town called Condega to help a women's construction team that was building a school. Hitchhiking is a risky way to travel, especially for a young woman in a foreign country that was (oh yeah) in a civil war. But since most of the country's trains and buses were inoperable, a ride from strangers was often the only transportation available. So there I stood, thumb out, by the side of the Pan American highway, as car after bus after truck whizzed by me, tossing another layer of light-brown dust onto my once-white Reebok sneakers. Dozens of other people were also along this half-mile stretch of road hoping for a ride, including some soldiers. After about two hours of waiting in the relentless tropical sun, a large military pickup truck slowed down near me to let on the soldiers. Along with those soldiers and a few other civilians, I managed to scramble onto the back of the truck. And we proceeded north through enemy territory.

As I sat cross-legged on the floor of the truck's pickup bed, jostling alongside twenty young men wearing camouflage khakis and toting machine guns, it dawned on me that taking this ride might not have been such a bright idea. But what could I do, now in a desolate stretch of mountain road, except keep going? After a half-hour of blessedly uneventful driving, the mood suddenly switched. The soldiers who had been casually seated alongside me became instantly attentive. Someone had spied activity in the hills. My military riding companions pulled around the guns that had been slung over their backs and grasped them in ready position. The truck slowed to a stop and the soldiers jumped out. My heart pounding, my mind turned, of course, to my Old Testament class.

25. Liberation theology is a Christian theological movement that emerged from Latin America in the late 1960s, maintaining that God is on the side of the oppressed.

I recalled my professor at Union Theological Seminary, Dr. Phyllis Trible, comparing translations of Psalm 121. Dr. Trible explained that the first verse of the King James Version: "I will lift up mine eyes unto the hills, from whence cometh my help," could imply that deliverance comes from the mountains themselves. Understanding nature to have a soul is animism and not the belief of the Hebrew Bible. More likely, she suggested, enemy soldiers were in those hills.

Now watching the men in camouflage clothes disappear into the brush and hearing gunshots, I prayed as the thumping in my chest increased:

> I lift up my eyes to the hills
>> [there are enemy soldiers in those hills]—
>> from where will my help come?
> My help comes from the LORD,
>> who made heaven and earth. (Ps. 121:1–2)

Fearing for my life, I connected with my faith and found inner strength through these words. "Trust," the psalmist reminded me. I breathed deeply and my heart rate slowed, even as I heard one last shot and a man triumphantly yell, "Lo tengo! Lo tengo!" My eyes scanned the hillside until I spied the victorious soldier with his arm outstretched above his head, something large and long dangling from his hand. I was sure he held a dead enemy's gun, until he got closer to the truck with his prize. Which was an iguana. Nicaraguans eat these large lizards as a delicacy. While I had been thinking that I could be killed at any minute, the soldiers had been searching for supper. Mission accomplished, they climbed back in the truck, which resumed its rambling. Reptile blood trickled onto the floor of the truck bed, adding spots of crimson to my dusty Reeboks, as I thought of how Psalm 121 had helped me through an intense, scary experience. Shaken by fear, I held on to this psalm to steady myself. I used Psalm 121 as believers have looked to the psalms for millennia: as a vehicle for connecting with faith at any time and in any place. And you can use them that way too.

Like a caring friend, Psalms can help us feel less alone. Psalms and feminism both recognize and thereby validate a wide range of feelings for all people. Binary gender constructs, with firmly set ideas about how men and women should behave, limit acceptable emotions. Women can cry from sadness, but men should not. Men can get angry and express their wrath, but women should not. But men experience sorrow and women know fury. Men who get upset from troubles are often told to "buck up" and "take it like a man." Women who get mad at offenses are often told to "take a joke" or that an insult was "nothing personal." This strategy protects the offender by removing responsibility for the harm inflicted and placing blame on the person who was demeaned. Instead, feminism and Psalms affirm that how we are hurt or healed matters. Psalms and feminism hold to the truth that all people have valid, complicated emotions. Feminism and Psalms remind us that everything that affects a person is personal.

How could it be otherwise?

———— **Questions for Reflection and Conversation** ————

1. Listening to music can evoke powerful emotions. What kind of music do you enjoy? Why? How does it make you feel?

2. In Psalm 137, the psalmist is far from home. What is the farthest you have ever been from your home? What or who took you there? What was the experience like?

3. Sometimes the words we carry within us provide solace or guidance. What words or sayings offer strength or comfort to you? Where do they come from, and why do you remember them?

Song of Songs
in Sing Sing

The iron bars on the doors at Sing Sing Correctional Facility are thicker than your thumb. The keys are almost as long as your hand. Back in 1826, this maximum-security prison opened in Ossining, New York, along the Hudson, to house those from the city who were convicted of crimes and then "sent up the river." So as prisons go today, this one is low-tech. No electronic beeping through computerized locks here; rather, the sound of heavy metal on metal—*claaang claaang*—rang in my ears as I walked into Sing Sing.

God had pulled me, steadily, invisibly, to those thick, iron-bar doors. I have no other way to explain my fierce and perplexing desire to teach inside prisons. I just know that one night, about ten years ago, I was tossing and turning in bed, feeling that God was calling me to this work. I glanced at the alarm clock (2:15 a.m.), then got out of bed to kneel in my pajamas at the bedside, hands folded in prayer (not something I do often). "Okay, God," I silently relented, "I'll teach in prisons. But you're going to have to help me." Who did I think I was, setting conditions before God? But Jacob does the same (see Gen. 28:20–22) and felt God's presence along his journey, so why not give it a try? My own life-altering experience began.

Ironically and appropriately, getting myself into prison took a lot of dedicated effort. Fingerprints, vaccination records, volunteer training, and months of waiting for a thorough security clearance finally allowed me to enter Sing Sing. I remember the first day walking into the space where I would teach: cement-block walls painted white, no windows, and a blackboard at one end. Books, pens, chalk: okay. PowerPoint, computers, internet: no way. Thirteen desks formed a U-shape, with the teacher's desk in the front. I was the sole woman and the only white, non-Hispanic person in the room. My students, all men wearing hunter green pants and shirts, were seated politely at their desks. The air was charged with expectation and eagerness, as it often is on the first day of school, while I was having an out-of-body experience. I felt like I was looking down on myself in some sort of show or movie: reverse *To Sir, with Love* meets *Shawshank Redemption*. The line from "I Have Confidence" in *The Sound of Music*, parodied in *The Book of Mormon*, came to mind but with my own twist: "Alone in a room with convicted felons . . . what's so fearsome about that?"[1] Walking to the front of the class, I somehow managed to trip over my teacher's desk. (A desk? Really? It's so large.) Little did I know how much love for each other and the Bible we would generate in that room. Teaching inside Sing Sing would become my Song of Songs.

Song of Songs, also called Song of Solomon or Canticles, is unique among biblical books. Read its eight chapters and you may wonder, "What are these erotic love poems even *doing* in the

---

1. When I first started teaching at Sing Sing, I used words like "convict," "felon," "prisoner," and "inmate." Recognizing the inherent denigration in such terms, I now use designations that start with the word "person," such as "person incarcerated," "person in prison," etc. See Bartley, "I Am Not Your Inmate."

Bible?!" The pages overflow with intimate sexual poetry. Song of Songs alternates between the main speaker, a woman expressing her burning passion, and her lover, the man who offers his own ardent devotion. They savor and celebrate each other. Marriage and childbearing merit no mention; theirs is pure, sensual joy. The lovers' exchanges are shared in a city, in a field, and beneath watchtowers, but mostly their words of lust linger in a lush garden. The air hangs redolent with cinnamon and myrrh; the tongue savors chewy, sweet raisins and crisp, tangy apples. Unlimited time with the person your heart fervently desires? Days spent in endless erotic bliss? Luscious surroundings fueling physical, emotional desire and cherished expressions of affection? It seems hard to imagine a starker contrast than that between Song of Song's fragrant, delicious, sensory delights and Sing Sing's hard gray walls, cages for humans, and institutional chow tables holding processed food in aluminum trays.

And yet, both Song of Songs and Sing Sing overflow with longing. Neither setting is overtly religious.[2] Both offer a realm filled with fervent feeling. Song of Songs and Sing Sing were formed by their cultural contexts and yet exist distinct from their wider worlds. People yearn to matter, to be loved. A focus on the body is central. And both Song of Songs and Sing Sing invite us to reexamine how we understand the Bible.

Over the past few years, I have given talks on prison and the Bible. Typically, a presentation takes place in a church basement: a large linoleum-floored room set up with a couple dozen folding chairs, a big metal coffee urn and a stack of paper cups in the back, a screen for the PowerPoint from my laptop in the front. I begin by asking the kind folks gathered if they can name anyone who commits a crime in the Bible. As they pause to think, I offer

---

2. Song of Songs is the only book of the Bible with no reference to God or religious life. Even though the book of Esther also does not explicitly mention God, Esther is a believing Jew who fasts as an appeal for God's help when her people are threatened (Esther 4:14–16). Song of Songs stays secular.

a clue: "Who are the two best-known individuals in the Old Testament and in the New Testament?" From Israel's beginning to the church's formation, people who kill others or violate the law are the Bible's most revered leaders.

The Israelites evolve from a family to a people with Moses as their guide in the book of Exodus. Working as slaves in Egypt, the Israelites are oppressed by Pharaoh and yearn for their deliverer (Exod. 1). Exodus 2 introduces Moses as the baby of an enslaved woman. He is saved by collaboration among girls and women: Moses' mother puts him in a basket among the reeds of the Nile; his sister watches over the basket; Pharaoh's daughter lifts him from the river; and Moses' sister arranges for Pharaoh's daughter to pay a Hebrew woman (Moses' mother) to nurse the child.[3] Moses spends his earliest years as a Hebrew and then as an Egyptian, bringing bicultural advantages to his later role negotiating with Pharaoh to lead the Israelites out of Egypt. But when Moses becomes an adult, his first independent action is to murder someone: "One day, after Moses had grown up, he went out to his people and saw their forced labor. He saw an Egyptian beating a Hebrew, one of his kinsfolk. He looked this way and that, and seeing no one he killed the Egyptian and hid him in the sand" (vv. 11–12).

Did they teach you *that* story in Sunday school? Moses clearly knows this act is wrong because he first looks to make sure no one is watching and then covers up the evidence! As a baby and very young child, Moses lived with his Israelite slave family, then he grew up as the son of Pharaoh's daughter, probably in a palace. This story resolves the question of where his allegiance lies. Without Moses, the Israelite people likely would have faded away in servitude. What if Moses had slain the Egyptian, then received the sentence for intentionally killing someone (murder in the first degree) in New York State? Twenty-five to life. What if Moses

3. For discussion of the girls in Exod. 2:1–10, see Betsworth and Parker, "'Where Have All the Young Girls Gone?'"

had gotten the sentence for killing an officer of the state in Texas? Death. The Bible would be a *really* short book.

David is the greatest king of Israel. His name in Hebrew means "beloved," which encapsulates how the Bible and most of its readers view him. David is celebrated throughout the Old Testament, where his name appears more than any other, except God. Unlike Moses, whose crime is spontaneous and arguably a crime of passion, David carefully crafts his plan to kill a man who has done nothing wrong. Indeed, David's homicidal victim is one of his own faithful soldiers.

In 2 Samuel 11, David sees a woman named Bathsheba bathing, purifying herself after her period. Some readers are surprised that the Bible bluntly brings up menstruation (see also Gen. 31:35), but we needn't impose any post-Victorian mores on a book that has no fear of sex (as in Song of Songs!). This detail is critical because David sends for Bathsheba, has sex with her without her consent, and then she becomes pregnant. The narrator pays no attention to Bathsheba's awful situation, that she will now bear a child of rape. Instead, the focus stays on David. The baby to be born is definitely his, but Bathsheba is married to Uriah, a soldier in David's army. David summons Uriah from the battlefield and repeatedly tries to get him to spend the night with his wife, but honorable Uriah will not indulge himself in such pleasures while his military comrades are enduring the hardships of the battlefield. With Machiavellian determination, David then gives Uriah a letter—containing his own death warrant—to take back to the commander. Uriah dutifully and unknowingly delivers this message that indeed leads to his being killed. With Uriah conveniently out of the way, David marries Bathsheba. This beloved king has worked assiduously to have his own loyal soldier expunged, but Bible readers do not think of David as the man who breaks half of the ten commandments.[4] *Not at all.* Instead, we remember

---

4. David murders Uriah, commits adultery, steals Bathsheba (another man's wife), bears false witness against Uriah, and covets a woman who is married, violating commandments five through ten (Exod. 20:13–17).

David as the hero of the David and Goliath story! David gave us the Psalms! He's the lover, poet, warrior, and king—Israel's ideal leader celebrated for millennia! And he is a sexual offender and premeditated murderer.

The New Testament also has those who commit crimes as its superstars, starting with Jesus Christ. Jesus is crucified—nailed to a cross—just like thousands of other condemned people who were executed under the Roman Empire. Jesus came from relatively humble beginnings in the occupied land of Palestine in the first century of the Common Era. Already his ethnic and societal status make him vulnerable. Calling further attention to himself, Jesus attracts followers through his teaching, healing, and preaching. He is accused of treason for claiming that he is a king. Jesus says nothing to deny these claims and so is sentenced to crucifixion—a purposely drawn out, painfully torturous way to die.

Crucifixion was reserved for those who were reviled, including slaves, foreigners, and the poor. Spikes were driven through the wrists and feet to hold the body to the wooden brace, which often included a small ledge as a seat, so the body didn't just rip off from the hands. People hanging on a cross would die from asphyxiation as their lungs eventually collapsed. The little seat helped to prolong the agony. Birds would pick at the rotting flesh. Christians look to Jesus and seek to learn how to live from his ministry. We look at his death and believe he accomplished salvation for others through his resurrection. But Jesus' experience as a condemned person also carries a troubling realization: our treatment of people who commit crimes can be inhumane.

Paul, the great apostle, would have known this well. He is perhaps more responsible than anyone else (including Jesus) for the birth of Christianity. Without him, knowledge of Jesus might have faded out after a generation or two, but Paul organized house churches and traveled throughout the Roman Empire to spread Jesus' message. As relayed in the book of Acts, Paul was a Pharisee (a sect of religious Jews; see Acts 23:6) who used to persecute Christians until a vision of the risen Christ told him to stop (9:1–9). He had a total change of heart, although probably not a "conversion" because, like Jesus, Paul stayed Jewish throughout his life. But now Paul worked to build communities of people who believed that Jesus was God's anointed. (The word for "anointed" is *meshiakh* [messiah] in Hebrew and *christos* [christ] in Greek.) Like Jesus, Paul was considered a troublemaker by the Roman state, which jailed him repeatedly.

Prisons in the ancient world were human holding pens that doubled as hellholes. People charged with crimes were often chained to walls at the neck, arms, or feet. The quality of your imprisoned life was determined by the length of your chain. Imagine if the chain around your neck prevented you from ever sitting or squatting, let alone lying down. (There were laws prohibiting chains that were too short, but the existence of such legislation shows that chain length was an issue.) Once people were tried, they would be released, beaten, tortured, exiled, or killed. Paul was repeatedly thrown into prison, where he wrote formal letters (called epistles) to communities of believers. Four books of the New Testament— Ephesians, Philippians, Colossians, and Philemon—claim to be written by Paul while he was in prison.[5] These epistles are foundational to the Christian faith. Throughout the Bible, readers depend on the stories and insights of people who commit crimes, some of whom are the founding fathers of Judaism and Christianity. But we do not remember Moses, David, Jesus, and Paul for the worst thing they have ever done.

In one of my church talks about prison and the Bible, a man in the audience challenged me. "You are making light of people

---

5. Scholars agree that the epistles of Romans, 1 and 2 Corinthians, Galatians, Philippians, 1 Thessalonians, and Philemon were all written by Paul. On the basis of writing style and content, many scholars question Pauline authorship of Ephesians, Colossians, and 2 Thessalonians. The letters of 1 and 2 Timothy and Titus (called the Pastoral Epistles) as well as the book of Hebrews are commonly attributed to Paul but were not written by him, since they address issues that surfaced after his lifetime.

who destroy others' lives!" he accused me. The atmosphere in the room, usually casual and friendly, instantly became charged with tension. I paused. He was right. And then I explained, "Listen, I get it. My parents were robbed of their life savings. You think, white-collar crime—no big deal, right? The stress of that loss led to my mother's sudden death of a heart attack a few months later." Since I was already struggling not to cry in front of a room of strangers, I didn't mention that the man who robbed my parents (and many others) spent their stolen money on his own defense lawyers and got a very light sentence. I did say that I recognize that some people's lives are forever, horribly, irrevocably damaged or even destroyed due to crime, and for that I am truly, deeply sorry. And I realize that the offense committed against my parents was not a physical assault and that violent crime creates even more trauma. Yet I still believe that no one—*no one*—is beyond God's mercy.

The Hebrew term for "mercy," *rakhamim*, reminds us that our physical and emotional selves are intertwined. People in prison know that what we experience corporeally connects to what we think and feel. Words in the Hebrew Bible convey this same awareness as terms suggesting emotions stem from the names of body parts. The verb *rakham*, meaning "to cause to love, have mercy, take pity on," is related to the Hebrew word for "womb" (*rekhem*), the life-giving center of the body's compassion.[6] The Hebrew word *yad* means "hand" and also "power." When we use our hands to heal or hurt, we embody our authority and ability. The slave girl Hagar is under her mistress Sarah's "hand"; she is also in her power (Gen. 16:6). The word *af* means "nose" or "nostril" and also "anger," as when an infuriated person's nostrils flare. When God is repeatedly described as being "slow to anger," the Hebrew used is *erekh appaim*, which literally means "long of nostrils"—good news because the hot air of fury has a long way

---

6. Koehler, Baumgartner, and Stamm, *Hebrew and Aramaic Lexicon*, 1216–18.

to go and can cool down before it reaches you.[7] The bowels, *meeh* in Hebrew, are the place of churning emotion (as in "I feel sick to my stomach"), sometimes translated as "anguish" (Jer. 4:19) or "heart" (Isa. 16:11). Later New Testament texts show the influence of Hellenistic thinking in which the body is subordinate or even opposed to the mind. Jesus reflects this dualism when he asks the disciples to stay awake with him: "The spirit indeed is willing, but the flesh is weak" (Matt. 26:4; Mark 14:38). But the Hebrew writers recognize that if your mind is stressed, your body feels it. If your body hurts, your spirit suffers.

The stories of our lives become encoded in our flesh; each one of us is a breathing narrative. Someone looks at you or me and, without even realizing it, creates a backstory for us of their devising, assuming your position or my worth. A few aspects of how we appear are those we usually choose, such as hairstyle, clothes, or body art, but most are not, such as height, shape, skin color, eye color, facial features, and disabling conditions. We are sized up in a glance, then treated according to another person's perception of *our own* reality, which may have little or nothing to do with your or my actual life.[8] We are judged—for better and for worse—before someone knows our story. Feminism points out the unfairness of these judgments and expectations, which are largely informed by culture. Too often, toxic messages, unspoken commands, and harsh assessments are laid upon our bodies, our selves.

"Be sexy!"

"Be tough!"

"You're dangerous!"

---

7. See Exod. 34:6; Num. 14:18; Neh. 9:17; Pss. 86:15; Joel 2:13; Jon. 4:2; Nah. 1:3, to cite a few of many examples.

8. Biblical scholarship also notes the various intersecting identities (regarding race, class, economics, nationality, education, etc.) that overlap in each person. For discussion of intersectionality in biblical studies, see Yee, "Thinking Intersectionally," 11–14; and Yee, *Hebrew Bible*, 1–38.

"Be quiet!"

"Be obedient!"

"Be skinny!"

"Show no emotion!"

"Smile!"

"Conform!"

"You're lazy!"

"You're strange!"

Look at the list above. Which of these silent, pervasive, and pernicious assessments and instructions does our culture direct at
women, children, men, transgender people, those who identify as
queer and nonbinary, and people of color? Not hard to figure out.
Feminism helps us notice how superficial evaluations can define,
limit, reward, command, and even punish people, just for looking
the way they do or being who they are.

Genesis 1:26–27 reminds us that all humans are created in God's
image: the nonbinary human (v. 26), and after that, male and female people (v. 27).[9] Each person *equally* reflects God's image.
No asterisk appears to make an exception. The theology is as
radical as God themself. You and I house a spark of God's love
inside our physical selves.

More than any place else in the Bible, the physical self takes
center stage in Song of Songs. Bodies bring delight—and danger.
Twice, the woman of the Song runs into sentinels, who patrol
the city's walls (Song 3:3; 5:7). (The Hebrew word translated as
"sentinels" is *shomerim*; these are the "watching ones," like prison
guards.) The first time, the woman is searching for her beloved
when the guards find her. She asks if they have seen the man she
seeks; she gets no response but quickly locates her beloved and

9. For further discussion, see "Beyond the Binary" on p. 152 in chapter 10 of this
book.

brings him home to her mother's house (Song 3:2–4).[10] Her first encounter with sentinels is harmless; the second is violent.

"I was asleep, but my heart was aroused" (Song 5:2a; translation mine). The woman longs for her lover. Just then, her beloved comes and knocks on her door, calling to her:

> Open to me, my sister, my love,
>> my dove, my perfect one;
> for my head is wet with dew,
>> my locks with the drops of the night. (v. 2b)

Dripping with desire, she opens to him (the door? herself? the Hebrew does not specify), but he is gone. So she goes to look for her lover and calls for him, but she receives no response (5:5–6). Without motivation, the guards find her, beat her, bruise her, and strip her of her veil (v. 7). So she calls out to her friends, the daughters of Jerusalem, to relay a message of desire to her beloved (v. 8). They ask her why this man is so cherished over others (v. 9), and she rhapsodically tells them, bringing the focus of this book back to its familiar territory (vv. 10–16). Song of Songs is its own realm of longing and love, but there are pockets of danger.

Sing Sing is its own realm of longing and danger, but there are pockets of love. My students were kind and generous to me. During our class break, one student would bring me a cup of (lousy prison) coffee, doctored to taste as good as possible (which was a challenge but helped by lots of creamer and sugar). Another would give me a snack of peanuts that he had purchased at the commissary with his own hard-earned money.[11] Occasionally, a student would connect a Bible passage with a story from his own

---

10. As noted in chap. 3, references to "her mother's house" appear just four times in the Old Testament, all in stories focused on girls and women (Gen. 24:28; Song 3:4; 8:2; Ruth 1:8).

11. People in prison get paid very little for their labor, generally well below a dollar an hour. See Sawyer, "How Much Do Incarcerated People Earn in Each State?"

life that was heartbreaking. The other men would listen with care and compassion, which is a real act of love.

We also joked together in that cement-block classroom. I remember one day when a student, Lawrence, told me that he had been talking on the phone with his wife about our class.

"I told her my favorite Bible verse," he said with a sly smile.

"Oh really? Which verse is that?" I asked.

"You don't want to know," he told me—and I could see where he was headed.

"I really do," I insisted, smiling back at him.

"It's okay."

"No, please, read it for us."

Lawrence took his Bible, and, as I had anticipated, turned to 1 Timothy 2:12.

"I permit no woman to teach or to have authority over a man; she is to keep silent."

I paused a beat, and then, with a dramatic flick of the wrist, threw my lecture notes on the floor, tossed back my head, and strode toward the door.

"*Goodbye*, gentlemen!"

We all burst out laughing.

But my little joke points to a truth that is not funny.

Some Christians maintain that this verse from 1 Timothy should prevent me from standing in the front of any classroom. Have they never had a teacher who was a woman from whom they learned, and whom they valued? They might maintain that the Bible's teachings are timeless. Do these readers rightfully expect to die if they work on the Sabbath (Exod. 31:14; 35:2)? Do they think parents should kill their child if that child curses at them (Exod. 21:15, 17; Lev. 20:9)? Do they anticipate being put to death for adultery (Lev. 20:10; Deut. 22:22)? Likely not. Others might say that they take the Bible literally. When someone makes this claim, my quick response is to cite Mark 10:21. "Jesus says to sell everything you have and give the money to the poor . . . and I notice you're still wearing clothes."

The insights, stories, or verses that you or I lift from the Bible as enduring truths stem from our own biases. Most any action or behavior can be justified by the Bible, depending on where one looks and how one interprets the text. More than a book, the Bible is a library of literature written over a span of one thousand years (the word "bible" means "books" [plural] in Greek); like any decent library, it contains a wide range of ideas, including contradictions. The unusual power of the Bible stems from people of faith who hold this collection as the sacred Word of God. Perhaps for you, as for me, the sections where we feel God speaking depend on our interests and understanding of God. The problem arises when we take a particular passage out of the Bible to harm someone else (or ourselves) or to deny them (or us) God-given equal humanity. Invariably, the point of view lifted from its biblical context agrees with one's own opinion. It's the darndest coincidence.

But the Bible is descriptive, not prescriptive. Its pages reveal the hopes and joys and challenges and anguish of people who lived thousands of years ago as they struggled to understand their relationship with God. The writers did not know that their words would last for millennia. They did not have in mind people yet unborn. You or I may believe that the Holy Spirit is behind the formation and compilation of the Bible's words but then remember that the Holy Spirit is about the business of spreading God's grace. The Bible is not the culprit here. Those who abuse the Bible for their own controlling or damaging agendas are the ones to be challenged. When words of the Bible are used in hurtful ways, we can refuse to accept interpretations that go against the power of love that is God.

Sometimes parts of the Bible can be so painful or so personal that they are tough to discuss. Ironically and appropriately, I barely talked about Song of Songs when I was teaching in Sing Sing. Honestly, as the only woman in the room, I just felt uncomfortable speaking about this sensuous text. I'm sure there are ways to get to the heart of erotic love poetry in such situations without feeling awkward, but I did not know them. Even during our limited class conversation on this book, one student sighed deeply. Wistfully he looked up, as if searching for memories in his mind and confided, "Ah, it's been a long time, Dr. Parker . . ."—since he had had sex, was the clear subtext. Once more I was reminded of the Bible's profound ability to connect with our deepest human feelings: longing, loneliness, the craving for human touch, the desire to be loved.

Teaching the Bible in Sing Sing aroused love within me. I fell in love, yet again, with this confounding, complicated, conflicted body of texts. I realized that the Bible is brave—braver than I was in those moments in the prison classroom—to speak to the intimate truths of our lives. This collection of ancient literature not only reaches out to our spirits, hearts, and minds but also embraces our bodies. In celebrating all of our humanness, the Bible calls us to be humane: respecting each other, no matter who we are—even those of us who are too often neglected, forgotten, or even reviled—including people (like Jesus) who spend time in prison.

———————— **Questions for Reflection and Conversation** ————————

1. The setting for most of Song of Songs is a beautiful, lush garden where joy abounds. What places evoke joy in you? Why are they special?

2. When have you been in a situation where you stood out due to your race, gender, religion, sexuality, or some other part of your identity? What did you experience? How did it feel?

3. Moses, David, Jesus, and Paul are recognized as great leaders in the Bible, despite their crimes. Whom do you know or admire who has achieved greatness despite a challenging past? What have you accomplished despite obstacles?

9

My Favorite Feminist Jew

Until I got to college, I had hardly any Christian friends. It wasn't that I avoided or disliked Christians, being one myself; I just didn't know that many at my overwhelmingly Jewish public school. As soon as my family moved to the Five Towns community on Long Island when I started eighth grade, it became clear we were a religious minority.

A specific encounter stands out. In social studies we were learning about US history (read: accounts of wars and the accomplishments of mostly wealthy Caucasian men in North America). Our teacher explained that those who first got off the boats from Europe and came to this continent were WASPs.

A hand went up. "Wasps? Like bees?"

No, the teacher specified, WASP stood for "White Anglo-Saxon Protestant."

I thought, "My tribe."

Another girl raised her hand. "Are there any of those alive today?"

It seemed that my peers in this school had no clue what a "Protestant" was. This impression was confirmed a few days later when a classmate turned around in his chair and started asking me (the new girl) a slew of questions before class started.

"So, are you Jewish?" he asked (the obvious assumption).

"No," I told him.

"Catholic?"

"No."

Long pause.

"Muslim . . . ?"

I had never met a Muslim person then (to my knowledge), and I doubt he had either. My classmate just could not think of another religious option besides Jewish, Catholic, or Muslim.

I soon learned that the school population largely consisted of grandchildren of European Jews who had had the vision, resources, and connections to escape Hitler's death machine before it was too late. Through my new friends, I came to love and appreciate Jews and Judaism while remaining a devout Christian. Perhaps it shouldn't be a surprise, then, that I teach the Hebrew Bible to Christians preparing for ordained ministry.

Christians often forget that Jesus' sacred texts were the Hebrew Scriptures. Jesus was thoroughly Jewish—his texts, his traditions, his friends, and his family were all Jewish. The names of Jesus and his parents reflect this heritage. Jesus is named after Joshua, a name derived from the Hebrew root word *yasha*, which means "to deliver" or "to save."[1] Joshua *delivers* people to the Promised Land; Jesus *saves* people from their sins. (In its Aramaic context, the name "Jesus" means "he saves.") Jesus' mother, Mary, is named for Miriam, the sister of Moses. Both are teenage girls who take risks that ensure the life and safety of the baby boy in their family (Exod. 2:1–10; Luke 1:26–38). Jesus' father, Joseph, is named after (wait for it) Joseph, the favored son of Jacob who receives a fancy coat. Both Josephs interpret dreams in which God leads

1. The name "Jesus" does not have the "sh" found in Joshua since Hebrew has the letter *shin*, which conveys this sound; Greek has no equivalent letter, so it uses a *sigma*, pronounced as "s."

them to save their families (Gen. 37:5–11; 41:1–42:9; 50:20–22; Matt. 2:13–23). If you had asked Jesus if he was a Christian, he might have said (in effect), "A wha . . . ?" The word "Christian" appears only three times in the entire Bible, and in none of the earlier New Testament books (see Acts 11:26; 26:28; 1 Pet. 4:16). The term didn't even exist during Jesus' lifetime, and how could it, as it named a movement that grew up around his death and resurrection? Rather, as a good Jew, Jesus' main mission was to immerse himself in *tikkun olam*, a Hebrew phrase that means "world repair" and refers to acts of social justice. This is great news for feminists.

To call Jesus a feminist is, of course, anachronistic, but then again so is most of our thinking about the biblical world. We graft our modern thoughts onto those of the ancient writers to figure out what they meant, even when we come from a time and place deeply foreign to that of the Bible. When I frame Jesus as a feminist, I simply mean that he cared about women and treated them as full people who deserve as much respect as men, which, to me, is the heart of feminism. Jesus eats with women, spends time with them, defends them, and values them as friends and even colleagues. Women are critical supporters of Jesus' ministry (see Luke 8:1–3) and part of his innermost circle.

Then why no women disciples? The Greek words for "disciple" are *mathētēs* (masc.) and *mathētria* (fem.) and simply mean "learner," as in "*mathe*matics." In two of the four Gospels, or "good news" books that tell of Jesus' life (Matthew, Mark, Luke, and John), we get a list of twelve disciples who were Jesus' followers. The Gospel writers are sure to include twelve disciples, as opposed to ten or twenty, say, to mirror the twelve tribes of Israel. But the names of "the twelve" vary among the different Gospels![2]

2. Mark, the earliest Gospel, was written about forty years after Jesus died and lists Simon Peter, James and his brother John (with the intriguing nickname "Sons of Thunder"), Andrew, Philip, Bartholomew, Matthew, Thomas, James son of Alphaeus, Thaddaeus, Simon the Cananaean, and Judas Iscariot (Mark 3:16–19) as

The identity of the disciples appears not to matter as much as the number recorded. Jesus had many more "learners" who followed him, in addition to a group whose members change depending on the biblical book. The presence of women disciples is casually attested in Acts 9:36: "And in Joppa there was a disciple [*mathētria*] whose name was Tabitha, which interpreted is Dorcas. She was full of good works and acts of mercy that she did" (translation mine). The same word that denotes the men close to Jesus appears in the feminine form to matter-of-factly describe a woman.

Nonetheless, the maleness of Jesus' disciples or of Jesus himself is frequently used to deny women recognized positions of power within churches. I recall discussing the arguments used against women's ordination in a class at the Seminario Bíblico in San José, Costa Rica, where I studied for a semester of my seminary career. The professor was reviewing the book *Ecclesiogenesis* by Leonardo Boff. A world-renowned liberation theologian and former priest, Boff critiques the arguments of his Roman Catholic tradition, which does not ordain women, including the view that ordained leaders need to be in the image of Jesus.[3] If taken literally, this limitation leaves only brown-skinned Palestinian Jews as potential priests. If not taken literally, the doors can open wide. In our class discussion, I wanted to add that the Catholic Church ordains people of various races and abilities, including those who are physically disabled. Since I did not know the Spanish word for "handicapped," I tried what I often did, which was to say the French word that I did know (*handicapé*) with a Spanish accent. Plowing ahead, I spoke of those who were *handicapado*. My classmates chuckled. Since *handicapado* is not a word that exists in Spanish, my student colleagues understood the part they knew:

---

the twelve disciples. Matthew uses this same list (Matt. 10:2–4). Luke makes no mention of Thaddeus but instead inserts "Judas, son of James," sometimes called Jude (Luke 6:16; see also Acts 1:13). John substitutes Nathanael for Bartholomew (see John 1:45–48; 21:2).

3. Boff, *Ecclesiogenesis*, 76–97. See also Tamez, "Religión, género y violencia."

capado, which, it turns out, means "castrated." (That was a new vocabulary word I've never forgotten.) The point is that churches that do not ordain women ordain all kinds of other people who do not resemble Jesus. Perhaps something else is at play besides the Bible.

Instead of fringe characters who never take center stage, women are critical figures in Jesus' life and ministry. According to Luke 1, Jesus' mother, Mary, receives angelic news that she, an unwed mother, will bear a child (Luke 1:26–34). Betrothed to Joseph but not married, the scandalous implications of being pregnant could have cost Mary her life (see Deut. 22:22). But the young teenage girl who hears the angel Gabriel's annunciation courageously agrees to bear and birth baby Jesus (Luke 1:35–38). Mary's theology proclaiming a radical reversal of the social order, which she extols in a psalm we know as the Magnificat (vv. 46–55), is echoed in Jesus' preaching.[4] Where did Jesus' theology come from? Where does your understanding of God come from? Did your mother play a role in forming your faith? It seems likely that Mary's beliefs about God influenced Jesus as he grew. Interestingly, Jesus' father, Joseph, never speaks in the Gospels, perhaps to downplay his role as father and replace him with God. Joseph also does not appear in any stories of Jesus' life as an adult, maybe because he was no longer alive when his son was grown. But the woman who brought Jesus into the world is there when he leaves it (John 19:25).

Women are among Jesus' best friends. Compare the stories of Mary and Martha with the references to Thaddaeus or Bartholomew (among "the twelve"), about whom the Gospels give no specifics. These two sisters are close to Jesus. Perhaps the most famous story of the three of them together comes from Luke 10:38–42 when Jesus goes to Martha's house. While her sister

---

4. Jesus' theology of a reversed social order is explicit in Luke 6:20–26 (from the Sermon on the Plain; Luke 6:20–49) and Matt. 5:3–12 (from the Sermon on the Mount; Matt. 5–7). Luke 1:53 (from Mary's Magnificat) and 6:21, 26 (from Jesus' Sermon on the Plain) both envision the poor being raised and the hungry being filled.

Mary sits at Jesus' feet and listens to him, Martha is "distracted with many tasks" (v. 40), although the Greek word translated as "tasks" is a form of *diakonia*—meaning "office and work of a deacon," "ministry," and "service."[5] While translators portray Martha as a busybody, the Greek text shows her engaged in work that matters. Commentators frequently suggest that she has been preparing a meal for Jesus as a guest in her home, which is also a meaningful act of service. Mary sits at Jesus' feet listening to him, and Martha is frustrated because her sister is not helping her. Worried with all she needs to do (the word *diakonia* appears again, again translated as "many tasks" in the NRSV), Martha asks Jesus to intervene (v. 40). Jesus instead pronounces that Mary has chosen "the better part, which will not be taken away from her" as she learns from Jesus (v. 42).

This story has bothered me because I have been compared to Martha with some frequency. I have two younger sisters, Kate and Valerie; Kate and I studied for the ministry together. Just over one year apart in age, we started and graduated from the same seminary at the same time and were ordained in the same service. (My father was once asked what the chances were of Valerie going to seminary, to which he replied with a genuine smile, "Well, one hates to use it, but the word 'impossible' does spring to mind.") As two sisters seeking to live into our own ways of discipleship, Kate and I apparently invited the comparison to Mary (Kate) and Martha (me) among our seminary colleagues. Kate was centered and focused. I, on the other hand, often seemed over-burdened. I lugged around large stacks of books, scurrying between the wide, wood study table in the library, my tiny dorm room that mice periodically liked to visit, and the noisy, worn shelter for homeless women in Midtown where I worked, appearing "distracted by many tasks." Because of our association, when I hear this story from Luke's Gospel, my sympathy flies to Martha.

5. Abbott-Smith, *Manual Lexicon*, 107.

Jesus appears to belittle her request for help, which doesn't seem fair.

Early feminist scholarship appreciated this passage in Luke 10:38–42 and Jesus' words in defense of Mary. She has chosen to learn as a disciple sitting at the feet of her rabbi and Jesus protects her right to education. Luke's Gospel was also lauded as a textual goldmine with forty-two passages related to women, twenty-three of which are not found in any of the other Gospels.[6] But Jane Schaberg urges feminist readers to examine these stories critically. Schaberg suggests that the Gospel of Luke and the book of Acts, which were written by the same author, subtly extol women in silent, subservient roles, like Mary sitting wordlessly at Jesus' feet.[7] And why pit the sisters against each other?

John's Gospel affirms Martha and her close relationship with Jesus.[8] John 11:5 simply states, "And Jesus loved Martha and her sister and Lazarus" (translation mine), perhaps suggesting that he was closer with the sisters than the brother. When Lazarus gets sick and then dies, Jesus goes to their town of Bethany (vv. 17–18). Martha comes to meet him and professes her faith in Jesus' abilities as a wonder-working prophet, even though her brother has now been dead for four days (vv. 20–22). Jesus proclaims that Lazarus will rise again, which Martha understands as a reference to the resurrection (vv. 23–24). When Jesus asks if she believes in his power to offer eternal life (vv. 25–26), Martha boldly professes her faith: "Yes, Lord, I believe that you are the Christ, the son of God, the one coming into the world" (v. 27; translation mine). After raising Lazarus from the dead (vv. 41–44), Jesus later celebrates Passover with Martha, Mary, and Lazarus

6. Schaberg, "Luke," 367.
7. See also the updated version of Schaberg's chapter on Luke: Schaberg and Ringe, "Luke."
8. This reading follows John 11 as it appears in our Bibles. However, recent scholarship from Elizabeth Schrader questions if Martha was a sister of Lazarus (Schrader, "Was Martha of Bethany Added?"). See the section "Martha, or More Mary?" on p. 155 in chapter 10 of this book.

(12:1). Again, Martha ministers (*diēkonei*) to Jesus (v. 2). Drawing on further documents from ancient Christian communities, Gail O'Day proposes that Martha was known as "Martha the *diakonos*" ("the minister"), like Phoebe, another woman recognized as a *diakonos* (Rom. 16:1).[9] Women like Martha and Mary were part of Jesus' innermost circle, ministering to him in his life and there with him at his death.

Jesus' death and resurrection is the central event of the Christian faith, yet the four Gospels differ in their accounts. Who first came to the place of Jesus' burial and discovered that the tomb was empty? Was it Mary Magdalene, Mary the mother of James, and Salome (Mark 16:1)? Mary Magdalene and the other Mary (Matt. 28:1)? The women who had come from Galilee (Luke 23:55)? Or just Mary Magdalene (John 20:1)? Does an angel (Matt. 28:5–6) or a young man in a white robe (Mark 16:5–6) tell the women not to be afraid, for Christ has risen? Maybe two men talk to the women at the tomb (Luke 24:4–5)? Or does Jesus himself appear at the sepulchre site, as Mary first mistakes him for a gardener (John 20:13–16)? Discovering the risen Christ is arguably the most monumental occurrence not only in the Gospels but in the history of Christianity. And one critical point on which Matthew, Mark, Luke, and John agree is that women were the first witnesses to their risen savior.

If you were to ask most people about women who were friends of Jesus, they'd probably mention Mary Magdalene. If you asked them about Mary Magdalene, they'd tell you she was a prostitute.[10] Why? They might recall the rock opera *Jesus Christ Superstar* or remember a story from the Gospels where a woman washes Jesus' feet with her hair and he forgives her sins. This idea of Mary Magdalene as a whore has a strong hold on our collective imagination.

9. O'Day, "Martha," 115.
10. Understanding Mary Magdalene as a sinner and Mary, the mother of Jesus, as a saint plays into the patriarchal platforms that place women in the pit or on a pedestal.

But Mary Magdalene is one of the leading figures in the Gospels. Whenever women are mentioned surrounding Jesus, her name appears first (except in John 19:25, where her name comes after those of Jesus' mother and aunt).[11] In all four Gospels, she is there to discover the empty tomb (Matt. 28:1–10; Mark 16:1–10; Luke 24:1–10; John 20:1–18). The Gospel of Peter (GP), an early Christian text that is not in our Bible, describes Mary Magdalene as a disciple of the Lord (*mathētria tou kyriou*; GP 12:50).[12] Medieval preaching commonly referred to Mary Magdalene as the "apostle to apostles."[13] But that is not how most people know her today. Why the need to define women in relation to men? Why focus on sexuality in telling women's stories?

When I was beginning the ordination process, one of the first steps was to talk with a committee that would help discern my call to ministry. In advance of this meeting, I had written and distributed theological statements in response to historical questions of my Methodist tradition about God's love and grace in my life and my service to the church. The evening when the committee gathered in a small church meeting room, I verbally summarized these documents. After pouring out my ecclesiastical heart and theological soul, I sat in a metal folding chair feeling very vulnerable while waiting for questions about the invisible pieces of my innermost self that I had laid out before the committee members. After a moment or two, an avuncular middle-aged man with a full head of gray hair began the discussion. "So," he asked, "do you have a boyfriend who shares your views?" "Excuse me?" I thought but did not say. "How is that question relevant to *anything* I just said?" None of the other five committee members spoke up to

11. Osiek, "Mary 3," 121.
12. The Gospel of Peter likely was written in the latter part of the second century. Henderson, *Gospel of Peter*, 42. For comparison of the GP with Gospel accounts of the empty tomb, see pp. 197–202.
13. For full discussion of Mary Magdalene as the *apostolorum apostola*, including images from medieval art, see Jansen, *Making of the Magdalen*, 62–82.

point out the disconnect, so after waiting a moment, I made some general deflective comment like, "I have lots of friends with different views" and smiled and left it at that. Why the need to define women in relation to men? Why focus on sexuality when hearing women's stories? Asking if I had a boyfriend was irrelevant to my call to ministry, just as viewing Mary Magdalene as a prostitute is irrelevant to hers. There is nothing about sex in her biblical story. So where does the idea of her promiscuity come from?

Not the Gospels. Rather, an Easter sermon given by Pope Gregory I in the sixth century links the unnamed woman in Luke 7, who washes Jesus' feet with her hair and is forgiven for her sins, with Mary Magdalene in Luke 8.[14] But the Bible itself never makes this association.

Luke 7:37–50 tells of a woman who seeks Jesus when he is at the home of a Pharisee named Simon. She brings an alabaster jar of ointment, which she pours on Jesus' feet, washing them with her tears and drying them with her hair. The Pharisee thinks to himself that Jesus should know "what kind of woman this is who is touching him" (v. 39), an impression no one in the story (including the narrator) confirms. Apparently sensing the Pharisee's judgment, Jesus offers a parable in defense of the woman about a creditor forgiving debts (vv. 40–46). While this unnamed woman has been introduced as a sinner (Greek: *hamartōlos*), nowhere in this story does the Greek word for prostitute (*pornē*) appear. News flash: women can lie, steal, cheat, and commit all kinds of sins that have nothing to do with sex! The word *hamartōlos* is a general term for those who are not righteous, also used to refer to Simon Peter (5:8), a repentant tax collector (18:13), and Jesus himself (John 9:16). Does anyone suggest that *they* are loose sexually?

Luke's introduction of Mary Magdalene comes after this footwashing episode, but the writer makes a point of first leading the reader to another time and place, then refers to the casting out

14. King, "Canonization and Marginalization," 285.

of demons when introducing "Mary, the one called Magdalene" (Luke 8:2; translation mine). Elizabeth Schrader and Joan Taylor suggest that "Magdalene" is not the name of a town but rather an epithet or designation. Usually the nicknames of his friends are given by Jesus, as with the disciple Simon, who is known as Peter, which means "rock."[15] The word *magdalēnē* (Magdalene) comes from an Aramaic root meaning "make great, magnify." In Greek, Jesus' good friend is not simply Mary Magdalene but *maria hē magdalēnē*: literally "Mary *the* Magdalene." Mary's designation as "the Magdalene" indicates her significance and could be translated as "the tower" (fem.) or "the magnified one."[16] Instead interpreters drag down and sully the textual portrait of Mary Magdalene, characterizing her as a prostitute. Yet we more accurately raise up Mary the Magnified One as the apostle who witnesses to the resurrection and stands as a towering presence in the Gospel tradition.

We know that women remained prominent in early Christian communities because writers to these communities specifically address issues of women's leadership and roles in the home.[17] These notorious texts are included in the "household codes" that seek to establish hierarchies that run counter to the egalitarian Jesus movement.[18] Spreading the word about Jesus' resurrection, the apostle Paul sought to abolish binary divisions among the faithful: "There is no longer Jew or Greek, there is no longer slave or free, there is no longer male and female; for all of you are one in Christ Jesus" (Gal. 3:28). But, unfortunately for feminists, other Christian writers after Paul missed the memo.

---

15. For further examples, see Schrader and Taylor, "Meaning of 'Magdalene,'" 753.

16. Schrader and Taylor, "Meaning of 'Magdalene,'" 751, 756, 761, 773. See also Jastrow, *Dictionary*, 726.

17. See Col. 3:18–4:1; Eph. 5:22–33; 1 Pet. 3:1–6. As Carolyn Osiek notes, those who defend the hierarchy of men and women in these texts put themselves in the position of defending the master/slave relationship that these passages also affirm. Osiek, "Household Codes."

18. Schüssler Fiorenza, *In Memory of Her*, 140–54. See also her more recent treatment of the household codes in Wo/men, *Scripture, and Politics*, 20–27.

When I teach the "household codes," I begin with a PowerPoint slide showing an article purportedly from a 1950s magazine called *Housekeeping Monthly*. (While the veracity of this publication is disputed, the advice promulgated for women nonetheless reflects the cultural ethos of this time.) The image shows a white nuclear family, with everyone playing their societally expected roles: father in a suit, tie, and collared shirt coming into the kitchen after work; mother in a dress, apron tied tight around her thin waist, wearing high heels and smiling at her husband while making dinner on the stove; and an adorable son and daughter blissfully playing between their parents. The accompanying text offers instructions on ways that wives should subject themselves to their husbands ("let him talk first," "never complain," "don't question his judgment," "make the evening his," etc.). After showing this slide, which I label "Household Codes for Wives 1955," I invite the students to divide themselves into groups according to gender identification: male, female, and nonbinary. Each group is to come up with their own "Household Codes for Husbands Today." I then record their suggestions on the classroom whiteboard. As I do this, the students quickly realize that each group creates different guidelines for what a model husband should do, and these ideas change according to time and culture. I have had groups dictate instructions like "help with the housework" and "allow the wife to have a career." I found myself unable to let these statements go unchallenged. "Help" with the housework? How about "share" the housework? "Allow" her to have a career?? Maybe "support and encourage her career choice"? In a small but significant way, my role as a scribe was like that of biblical scribes. The person doing the writing has an often overlooked but powerful say in supplying the words that are recorded, and perhaps passed on.

We only know Jesus through the words about his life that have been passed on to us. But through the thick lenses of distant time and foreign culture, I still clearly see a man who cared about all people, especially those who were given a hard time in the world, including women. In this way, the love that Jesus shared accords with the essence of feminism.

Jesus is my favorite feminist Jew, and Gloria Steinem (whose father was Jewish) is also on the list.[19] This feminist pioneer observes, "The first problem for all of us . . . is not to learn, but to unlearn. We are filled with popular wisdom of several centuries just past, and we are terrified to give it up."[20] Along with popular wisdom of ages gone by, we are also filled with damaging ideas about women traced to the Bible that many people hesitate to cast off. But liberation is at the core of both testaments. At the heart of the New Testament is a verse from the Old Testament: you shall love your neighbor as yourself (Lev. 19:18; Matt. 22:39; Mark 12:31; Luke 10:27), which is a profoundly feminist assertion.

Feminism and the Bible are not at odds with each other. Yes, women have been fed words of the Bible to nurture toxic thinking about their own supposed inferiority. But it is the feeders, not the scriptural food, at fault. No one should shove Bible verses down someone else's throat to make them choke, shrink, or suffer. Rather, we pick up the Bible to see what is good food for the soul, delights the senses, and is desired to make us wise. We partake of the Scriptures that open our eyes to the ancient cultures of the Bible while providing insight and offering wisdom for our modern lives. We are strengthened by spiritual sustenance as we blaze our own footpaths, Bible in hand, through this beautiful, terrible, wonder-full world. Scripture and feminism propel us forward as we leap to freedom.

19. Pogrebin, "Gloria Steinem."
20. Steinem, "New Egalitarian Lifestyle," 37.

──────── **Questions for Reflection and Conversation** ────────

1. Jesus gave nicknames to his friends. What nickname have you had? Who gave it to you? Do you like the nickname? Why or why not?

2. Mary and Martha are among Jesus' close friends. Who is a friend you cherish? Why?

3. Sometimes what we unlearn is more important than what we learn. What have you been taught that did not feel true to your experience or that served someone else's interest at your expense? How did you discover a truth that differed from what you had been told?

Curious, Like Eve?
Learn More

This section of the book shows that I meant it when I said that I know you are smart (p. 7).

The following eight sections correspond to chapters 2–9, arranged in the same order. Each academic excursus, or detailed discussion, explores a point made in the corresponding chapter. Through a closer look at issues of translation, life in the biblical world, and aspects of ancient Near Eastern culture, I share information that I find fascinating, and I hope you will too. A few of the sections use Hebrew and Greek letters so you can see close work with the original languages. One of the sections includes images, and another is an interview with a scholar whose work on women in the Gospels is gaining widespread recognition. Some of the forthcoming insights may surprise you, but all are grounded in solid scholarship and add deeper dimensions to our understanding of the Bible.

Misleading Translations of Genesis 3:6 and 3:16 (chap. 2)

While both Adam and Eve are in the garden and eat the fruit of the tree of knowledge of good and evil, most people understand this disobedience to be Eve's fault. Many readers do not realize that Adam is standing right there when Eve takes the fruit because some English Bibles omit translation of one critical Hebrew word (in bold below).

Genesis 3:6

ותרא האשה כי טוב העץ למאכל
וכי תאוה־הוא לעינים
ונחמד העץ להשכיל
ותקח מפריו ותאכל
ותתן גם־לאישה **עמה** ויאכל

Transliterated and translated (with emphasis added), this verse reads:

vattere	*haishah*	*ki*	*tov*	*haets*	*lemaakhal*
And when she saw	the woman	that	good	the tree	for food
vekhi	*taavah-hu*	*laenayim*			
and that	delight-it	to the eyes			
venekhmad	*haets*	*lehaskil*			
and pleasant	the tree	to make wise			
vattiqqakh	*mippiryo*	*vattokhal*			
so she took	from its fruit	and she ate			
vattitten	*gam-leishah*	***immah***	*vayyokhal*		
and she gave	also-to her man	**with her**	and he ate		

The word *immah*, meaning "with her," is undisputed in the Hebrew text and appears consistently in all the earliest translations of the Hebrew Scriptures, starting from before the turn of the

Common Era. These include the Septuagint (Greek), the Targums (Aramaic), and the Peshitta (Syriac).[1] The first translation missing the words "with her" from Genesis 3:6 is the Latin Vulgate, rendered from the Hebrew by Jerome. An early Christian scholar and translator, Jerome lived and wrote during the fourth to fifth centuries CE. While his Bible translations usually remain close to the original texts, he frequently loses this objectivity in passages related to women, casting them in a negative light.[2] Continuing the trend, approximately one-third of all English Bibles from Jerome's time to our own leave out the words "with her" from this verse, making it easy to blame Eve alone for eating from the tree of knowledge of good and evil.[3]

Jerome's Latin translation of Genesis 3:16 has also altered the original Hebrew in ways that are detrimental to women.

Genesis 3:16

אל־האשה אמר הרבה ארבה עצבונך והרנך
בעצב תלדי בנים
ואל־אישך תשוקתך והוא ימשל־בך

el-haishah	amar		harbah	arbeh	itsvonekh	veheronekh
to-the woman	he said		great	I will make great	your labor	and your conception

beetsev	teledi	vanim
in labor	you will give birth to	children

veel-ishekh	teshuqatekh	vehu	yimshal-bakh
and to-your man	your desire/turning	and he	will rule-over you

1. The Septuagint dates from the third century BCE through the first century BCE; the Targums (or Targumim) date from the first through seventh centuries CE, and the Peshitta dates from the fifth century CE.
2. Barr, "Vulgate Genesis and St. Jerome's Attitude to Women," 269.
3. Common English Bibles that translate *immah* include the ESV, NASB, NJB, NKJV, NRSV, and NRSVUE; conversely, the MSG, NABRE, NIV, NJPS, NLT, RSV, and RSVCE are among those that make no mention of the man being "with her." For detailed discussion, see Parker, "Blaming Eve Alone."

Jerome rendered the punishment in Genesis 3:16 as, "I will multiply your toils and your conceptions; in grief you will bear children, and you will be under the power of your husband, and he will rule over you." This wording takes some worrisome liberties with the Hebrew and condemns the woman more than the text suggests, generating harmful ideas about women's roles in relation to men. Carol Meyers offers extensive analysis of Genesis 3:16, with close attention to the Hebrew vocabulary and phrasing. Her translation, fully supported in a close reading, begins, "I will make great your toil and many your pregnancies; with hardship shall you have children."[4] Giving birth is arduous work that women will endure in multiple pregnancies; the emphasis is on the strenuous task (*itsavon*), not on grief, as Jerome suggests.[5] The story is an etiology, or story of origins, explaining why women go through labor in childbirth.

The word Jerome gives as "power" is *teshuqat* and means "desire" or "longing."[6] The Septuagint, or Greek translation of the Hebrew Scriptures, understands *teshuqat* as "turning." Meyers suggests this "turning" means the return of the male and female person to their original oneness through sex.[7] If we translate *teshuqat* as "desire," Genesis 3:16b describes a woman's desire for sex. Women in the ancient world died about ten years before men on average because of death through childbirth.[8] For a woman to get pregnant meant she might die; without birth control, having sex was like playing Russian roulette. This mythical story can also be read as explaining why women would have sex despite risks. The statement that the man will rule over the woman also relates to sex, describing the male role as penetrator. Meyers translates

4. Meyers, *Re-Discovering Eve*, 102.
5. Koehler, Baumgartner, and Stamm, *Hebrew and Aramaic Lexicon*, 865. Forms of *itsavon* appear twice in Gen. 3:16 (*itsvonekh* and *beetsev*).
6. This word is relatively rare, appearing only two other times in the Bible: Gen. 4:7 and Song 7:10 (MT: 7:11).
7. Meyers, *Re-Discovering Eve*, 94–95.
8. Yamauchi and Wilson, "Childbirth and Children," 280.

the second part of the verse, "Your turning is to your husband, and he shall rule/control you [sexually]."[9]

While many Bible readers think that Genesis 3:16 forever ordains women be subject to men, the same readers never presume that Genesis 3:17–19 forever ordains men to be farmers who eat bread in sweat from relentless toil. When we understand women's roles as timeless but not men's, our failings perpetuate fallout from the text that has nothing to do with the text itself. Misogynist interpreters, not the Bible, create the tragic aftermath of a paradise that's lost.

The Status of Women in the Biblical World (chap. 3)

Perhaps you have heard that men had total control over women in the biblical world. Not so! Remarkably, women are considered full people. Of course, the Bible encompasses a wide range of varied literature and overwhelmingly focuses on men. Still, we can make some surprising observations and raise critical questions about the roles and status of women in the biblical world.

Both the Old and the New Testaments offer glimpses of women who have desires, dreams, agency, and ambition. In the Hebrew Bible, women feel lust and take pleasure in sex.[10] They wield public power as military commanders and as queens.[11] Women are explicitly called prophets and give counsel to kings.[12] In the New Testament, we encounter Jesus' mother, Mary, who proclaims that God radically reverses earthly power structures; this message becomes the theological foundation of her son's preaching.[13] Women are among Jesus' closest followers; they play key roles in

---

9. Meyers, *Re-Discovering Eve*, 102.
10. See Gen. 18:12; 39:6–12; Song 1:2–4.
11. See Judg. 4:4–9; 1 Kings 10:1–13; 19:1–3; 21:1–26; Esther 1; 5; 9.
12. See Exod. 15:20; Judg. 4:4; 2 Kings 22:14–20; Isa. 8:3; Neh. 6:14.
13. Matt. 5:3–12; Luke 1:51–53; 6:20–23.

his mission and bravely testify to his role as the Messiah.[14] In all four Gospels, women are the first witnesses to the resurrection.[15] Paul abolishes distinctions between male and female and raises up women as leaders in the church.[16] Women are not only integral but essential to the Bible's witness.

You: Then how come the Bible is so patriarchal?

Me: It's complicated. Let's see if I can make it easier . . .

First, the Bible was written over more than one thousand years. Culture changes over time. It is overly simplistic to make statements like "the Bible is patriarchal" and stop there, without defining what one means by "patriarchy."[17]

Second, while many biblical texts seek to place women in positions beneath men, we do not know if such regulations were followed, or how closely. If three thousand years in the future, someone were to read all our laws and presumed they were followed to the letter, they would imagine New York City with glittering, clean streets (littering is against the law) and highways where no one ever speeded beyond the posted limit (likewise illegal). Also, people today who raise up some dictums of the Bible as enduring, such as "wives, be subject to your husbands" (Eph. 5:22) simply ignore others, such as "slaves, obey your earthly masters" (6:5). Why one and not the other?

Third, remember that every translation includes interpretation. Like nearly all of the biblical writers, most Bible translators are men. Our English Bibles often convey readings that favor men and give them power, as in Ephesians 5:22 (cited above). The Greek here reads:[18]

---

14. Matt. 27:55–61; Mark 15:40–41; Luke 8:1–3; John 11:26–27; 19:25–27.

15. Matt. 28:1–10; Mark 16:1–10; Luke 23:55–24:10; John 20:1–18.

16. Rom. 16:1–15; Gal. 3:28; Phil. 4:2–3.

17. For fuller discussion on patriarchy in ancient Israel, see Meyers, "Was Ancient Israel a Patriarchal Society?"

18. This text follows NA[28], the standard Greek edition of the New Testament used by translators and scholars.

αι	γυναικες	τοις	ιδιοις	ἀνδρασιν	ὡς	τω	κυριω
ai	gunaikes	tois	idiois	andrasin	hōs	tō	kyriō
the	wives/women	to	their own	husbands/men	as	to the	lord

Admittedly, the context of Ephesians 5:22 focuses on hierarchy; still the Greek does not supply any verbs in this verse. The words "obey" or "be subject" have been added in by translators. Maybe married women should *love* their husbands as they also love the Lord. If you cannot read Hebrew and Greek (yet), you might compare different English versions or read an interlinear Bible that gives a direct word-for-word correlation. Translations can inaccurately foster ideas about female subordination.

Fourth, we need to examine the portrayals of women (or anyone) in the Bible. Instead of simply taking the text at face value, we ask who might have written this text and what agenda they were trying to promote. Why is something or someone represented or perceived in a certain way? You and I can read with a hermeneutic, or an interpretive lens, of suspicion. For example, multiple women in the Hebrew Bible appear desperate for sons (e.g., Sarah in Gen. 11:30; 16:1–2; 18:9–14; Leah and Rachel in Gen. 29:31–30:24). Did this fierce desire for male children come from the women who lived in ancient Israel, or do these concerns stem primarily from the minds of elite men who wrote with attention to male legacies? Of course, we cannot have definitive answers to these questions, but even raising them opens new possibilities for understanding biblical texts.

When you read the Bible, consider asking whose interests are served in a particular passage. Who benefits from a given translation or interpretation? At whose expense? Recognize and claim your own authority in making meaning from the Bible's words.

Goddesses of the Hebrew Bible and Ugaritic Literature (chap. 4)

The texts of the Hebrew Bible come from lands where belief in goddesses was strong. Three goddesses mentioned by name in the Bible—Asherah, Astarte, and Anat—play distinctive roles in Ugaritic literature.[19] Ugarit was a kingdom that existed north of Israel in the late second millennium BCE. This nation-state faded from history when it was conquered, around 1200 BCE. The texts from Ugarit were discovered around the mid-twentieth century and have a lot to teach us about the gods and goddesses in the land of Canaan.[20]

Asherah is the mother goddess in Ugaritic literature, where she is called Athirat. One of the narrative poems we have from Ugarit, the legend of Keret, tells of the king journeying to Athirat's shrine to make a vow and seek her help in getting a wife (*KTU* 1.14 iv 34–43).[21] Along with the patriarch of the pantheon, El, she reigns over the lesser deities (*KTU* 1.4 vi 46). El (which means "God" in Hebrew) and Athirat (or Asherah) form a couple, like the pairing of Yahweh and Asherah in the minds of some ancient Israelites.

Perhaps despite itself, the Bible gives evidence of Asherah's popularity. The root of her name, *asher*, means "happy" and is the name of one of the twelve tribes of Israel. The second son of Jacob and Leah's maid Zilpah (Gen. 30:12–13), Asher, has a name that may be theophoric, meaning it refers to a deity. Perhaps

19. Try to use the word "Ugaritic" in a sentence today, like "I recently learned about Ugaritic literature." People will be astounded at how intelligent you are. I'm not kidding. It's like a magic trick.

20. Canaan refers to the wider geographic region that encompasses Israel. For an introduction to Ugarit and its texts, see Coogan and Smith, *Stories from Ancient Canaan*.

21. The abbreviation *KTU* designates *Keilalphabetische Texte aus Ugarit*, the standard reference source for Ugaritic literature (edited by Dietrich, Loretz, and Sanmartín). These texts were written in cuneiform on clay tablets. Cuneiform is a type of writing made by pressing the tip of a reed into clay and forming groups of wedges that convey designations, words, or sounds. (Ugaritic is a Northwest Semitic language written in alphabetic cuneiform; each sign represents a distinct phonetic sound [or letter].) In the citation *KTU* 1.14 iv 34–43, the numbers 1.14 signify the tablet, iv is the column number, and 34–43 are the lines of that column. Not all tablets have multiple columns (see note 27), so every reference does not follow the same sequence.

the name of this son and tribe carries a tribute to the goddess Asherah.[22] In Judges 6:25–32, Gideon infuriates the people of his town when he cuts down their *asherah* pole, used to worship this goddess. In 1 Kings 15:13, the queen mother, Maacah, is deposed because of her image honoring Asherah. Second Kings 23:7 briefly notes that women in the Jerusalem temple were making cloth for Asherah, perhaps suggesting that she was a goddess of weaving.[23] Most of the Bible's references to Asherah, however, condemn cultic practices associated with her (e.g., 1 Kings 16:33; 2 Kings 13:6; 17:16; 18:4; 21:3; 23:15). She is a threat to the sole worship of Yahweh, and acts of devotion to her sacred pole were clearly *pole*mical (bad pun!).

Anat, another goddess of the region, shines in Ugaritic literature; in the Bible her portrayal is more opaque. Ugaritic narrative poetry, especially stories found on tablets known as the Baal cycle, shows Anat as a fierce young warrior goddess. She conquers mortal soldiers, defeats other gods, and rescues her partner god, Baal, from death (the god Mot).[24] In the Bible, a town seems named after her (*beth-anath*; mentioned twice in Judg. 1:33), and two other references loosely associate her with war and victory. Tantalizingly, Judges 3:31 simply names Anat (transliterated as Anath) as the mother (patron goddess?) of the judge Shamgar who saves Israel. Judges 5:6 gives another brief reference to Anat, with Shamgar as her son, within the poem known as "The Song of Deborah" (vv. 1–31). This text may be the oldest literary strand of the Bible, briefly carrying this young goddess to the biblical world before her influence slips away.

---

22. The tribe of Asher is eponymous, meaning it takes its name from a person.

23. The Hebrew in 2 Kings 23:7 says the women wove *battim*, literally "houses" for Asherah, which seems curious. Likely they made vestments or curtains or some other woven cloth for venerating the goddess. See Ackerman, "Asherah, the West Semitic Goddess of Weaving?"

24. See Dietrich, Loretz, and Sanmartín, *KTU* 1.3 ii; 1.3 iii 32–45; and 1.6 ii 30–37, respectively. For feminist discussion of Ugaritic literature, see Parker, "Women Warriors and Devoted Daughters."

Anat's sister in Ugaritic literature is Astarte, who is mentioned nine times in the Hebrew Bible.[25] Astarte is the Northwest Semitic name of Ishtar, the powerful goddess of war and love, revered in Mesopotamia. Astarte is a celestial deity[26] (conveniently, with the word "star" in her name). In Ugaritic texts, Astarte is paired with Anat in rituals that ward off snakes and fight hangovers! She is also associated with horses, war, hunting, and healing.[27] In the Bible, Astarte is repeatedly connected with Sidon, one of the major cities of Phoenicia, located north of Israel in modern-day Lebanon (1 Kings 11:5, 33; 2 Kings 23:13). In other occurrences, references to the "Astartes" come after mention of the "Baals," suggesting foreign goddesses parallel to foreign gods (Judg. 2:13; 10:6; 1 Sam. 7:4; 12:10). While the Hebrew Bible does not have a word for "goddess" (despite English translations that insert this word),[28] references to Asherah, Anat, and Astarte show that people worshiped them nonetheless.

Perhaps some ancient Israelites needed their faith in goddesses, who were part of their theological worldview, just as you or I might rely on our belief in God. Goddesses were revered in the land of Canaan long before the God of the Israelites was known. These established deities were not the outliers in the ancient Near East pantheon; rather, the new god, Yahweh, invaded their turf and, with help from the Bible writers, sought to take it over. Passionate

25. The name Astarte appears in the singular or plural. English translations sometimes give a different form from what appears in the Hebrew. The Hebrew conveys Astarte in the singular in 1 Kings 11:5, 33 and 2 Kings 23:13 and plural in Judg. 2:13; 10:6; 1 Sam. 7:3, 4; 12:10; 31:10.

26. van der Toorn, Becking, and van der Horst, *Dictionary of Deities and Demons*, 109–10.

27. For incantations against snakes, see Dietrich, Loretz, and Sanmartín, *KTU* 1.100 R20 and 1.107 V39. For dealing with effects of overdrinking, see *KTU* 1.114 V23. (The *KTU* numbers here indicate the tablet number [1.100, 1.107, and 1.114 respectively], followed by the side of the tablet [R meaning "recto" (front) or V meaning "verso" (back)] and the line number [20, 39, and 23 respectively].) For discussion of Astarte's roles changing over time in Northwest Semitic texts, see Schmitt, "Astarte," 216–19.

28. See 1 Kings 11:5, 33. The word translated as "goddess" is actually "gods" (*elohe*) in Hebrew.

teachings and prophetic warnings against venerating deities besides Yahweh inadvertently testify to tenacious belief in goddesses within the biblical world.

Children Can Be Prophets Too (chap. 5)

Unlike people, the Holy Spirit does not discriminate, as seen in the distribution of prophetic gifts. All kinds of people are prophets in the Bible and its surrounding world, as they are today. Prophetic gifts often surface in someone at an early age. Awareness of prophetic abilities can indicate a child's promise or enable these powers to be nurtured, as evident in varying times and in different cultures, including the Bible.

The academic study of children in the Bible is a relatively new field called "childist" biblical interpretation.[29] Just as feminist biblical interpretation focuses on women, childist interpretation explores and examines the lives of children in the biblical world to assess and appreciate their roles and importance. When we read the Bible through a childist lens, we notice the power children have and the perils they face as valuable and vulnerable members of their societies.

Four well-known prophets enter the biblical story as boys. The prophet Moses first appears as a crying child in a basket; the account of his rescue from a watery grave marks him as a person destined for greatness (Exod. 2:1–10). Samuel's story also begins auspiciously. When he is a child serving the priest, Eli, at the shrine of Shiloh, Samuel is called by the voice of God repeatedly during the night. Young Samuel receives a hard prophetic task, which he fulfills (1 Sam. 3:1–19). Similarly, God summons the boy Jeremiah to the role of a prophet (Jer. 1:4–10).[30] When Jeremiah objects

---

29. For an introduction to this field, see Parker, "Children in the Hebrew Bible" and "Engaging Studies."

30. The same Hebrew word, *naar*, describes Moses (Exod. 2:6), Samuel (1 Sam. 3:1, 8), and Jeremiah (Jer. 1:6, 7) and indicates people who are young, serve others, or both. For fuller discussion of this term, see Parker, *Valuable and Vulnerable*, 60–64.

that he is too young to talk well, God refuses to accept this excuse and reassures Jeremiah of their human-divine connection (1:6–8). Like Moses, Jesus' infancy is filled with drama (Matt. 2; Luke 2).[31] Like Samuel, Jesus is associated with a specific place of worship (1 Sam. 3:21; Luke 2:45–49). Like Jeremiah, Jesus shares his God-given insights while a boy (Jer. 1:6–8; Luke 2:46–47). The first time Jesus speaks is as a twelve-year-old child who amazes the teachers in the temple (Luke 2:41–47), revealing his prophetic gifts and understanding of God. Young Moses, Samuel, Jeremiah, and Jesus grow up to become central characters in the Bible's story, and their roles as prophets begin when they are children.

Predictably, prophetic girls are harder to find. Only one girl who is explicitly called "little" (Hebrew: *qetannah*) speaks in the entire Old Testament (2 Kings 5:2–3). She is an anonymous captured slave, whom scholars designate as the Israelite slave girl. While she does not act as a prophet herself, she tells her master's wife about the prophet in Samaria (Elisha) who could cure her afflicted husband, Naaman, of his leprosy. Believing the Israelite slave girl, Naaman undertakes the trip from Aram to Israel to see Elisha and eventually is cured (vv. 4–14). By suggesting that Naaman seek this prophet, the Israelite slave girl acts similarly to John the Baptist (e.g., Matt. 3:1–3, 11). Both play a part in leading others to a prophet with wonder-working abilities, including healing, multiplying food, and bringing the dead back to life.[32]

---

31. Jesus' mother is not married (Matt. 1:18–19; Luke 1:34); his parents each receive a visit from an angel foretelling Jesus' birth (Matt. 1:20–25; Luke 1:26–38); the angel tells of the child's power and glory (Luke 1:32–33); Jesus is born away from home in an animal stall (2:1–7); astrologers and shepherds pay homage to Jesus as a baby (Matt. 2:1–2, 9–11; Luke 2:8–20); a tyrant king wants to murder Jesus (Matt. 2:3, 7–8) and kills other baby boys in the attempt (vv. 16–18); his father learns via dreams how to keep his family alive (vv. 13–15, 19–23); baby Jesus is brought to the temple, where a devout man and a woman prophet affirm his role as the Messiah and redeemer of Jerusalem (Luke 2:22–40).

32. Examples of Elisha's wonder-working powers, cited above, are found in 2 Kings 5:1–14; 4:42–44; and 4:8–37, respectively. Similarly, Jesus heals people (e.g., Matt. 12:15; 14:14; 21:14; Mark 3:10; 6:56; Luke 5:15; 9:11; John 4:46–54; 5:11; 9:1–7), multiplies

Another slave girl in the Bible possesses her own prophetic ability. Acts 16:16–19 tells of Paul and his followers encountering an anonymous slave girl with spiritual gifts. While the NRSV reports that she has a "spirit of divination," the Greek is a bit more ominous, stating that she has a *pneuma pythōna* or "spirit of a python."[33] Scholars suggest that she may be demon-possessed, but her words are trustworthy. She calls out after Paul and his entourage, telling all who will hear, "These people are slaves of the God Most High, who declare to you a way of salvation!" (v. 17; translation mine). Not only does she speak this message of truth about the apostles, but her prophecies must have had merit since her owners profited from her abilities (v. 16). Yet Paul seems bothered by her, despite her honest affirmation, and commands the prophetic spirit leave her, which it does (v. 18).

Perhaps Paul feels threatened by the girl's abilities because she calls attention to him, marking him as a target. Indeed, this story concludes with Paul and his companion, Silas, being attacked and imprisoned, although this outcome is the result of Paul's own actions (Acts 16:19–23). Paul may have also felt threatened or rankled by this slave girl. She calls Paul and his companions "slaves" (*douloi*) of God, placing them on her societal level (v. 17). Some ancient manuscripts have her proclaim that the message of salvation is "for us," not "for you."[34] With this reading, a slave girl dares to claim Paul's hopeful message for herself and other slaves.

In the Bible, children are not only prophets but leaders (see Isa. 11:6). They don't appear in front of large crowds; instead,

---

food (Matt. 14:13–21; Mark 6:32–44; Luke 9:12–17; John 6:1–15), and revives the dead (Luke 7:11–17; 8:49–56; John 11:1–44). Like Joshua, Elisha and Jesus have names derived from the Hebrew root word *yasha*, meaning "to save" or "to deliver." (Elisha means "God saves.") Both Elisha and Jesus deliver people from illness, hunger, and even death.

33. Katy Valentine explains that this term "may refer directly to the Python serpent killed by Apollo at Delphi, a general term for a spirit of divination, or a ventriloquist." Valentine, "Reading the Slave Girl of Acts 16:16–18," 358n27.

34. The KJV translates the girl's words, "These men are the servants of the most high God, which shew unto **us** the way of salvation" (emphasis added).

they are those who lead by example. Reversal of expectations is a central theme in both testaments. Such a text invites us to discover wisdom from surprising sources, including children, and perhaps least expected of all, slave girls. Unlikely young prophets emerge from a biblical world where—like our own—anything is possible.

Job's Wife—Cursing or Blessing? (chap. 6)

In all forty-two chapters of Job, his wife utters only six Hebrew words. When Job loses his home, possessions, and children, she does too (a point the narrator completely ignores). According to the NRSV, Job's wife asks, "Do you still persist in your integrity?" then she commands, "Curse God, and die" (Job 2:9). Maligning interpretations of Job's wife are supported by translations that present a woman who dares to deride her husband and demean God—except her words in English are different from what we read in Hebrew.

In Job 2:9, the Hebrew has Job's wife making a statement, not asking a question.

ותאמר לו אשתו עדך מחזיק בתמתך
ברך אלהים ומת

Transliterated and translated (with emphasis added), we read:

vattomer	lo	ishto	odkha	makhaziq	betumatekha
she said	to him	his wife	still you	are holding on	to your integrity

barekh	elohim	vamut
bless	God	and die

The Hebrew grammar gives no indication of a question in the first part of the verse.[35] Rather, this phrase reads, "His wife said to him, 'You still are holding on to your integrity' [despite all

---

35. Questions in biblical Hebrew are generally indicated by the particle *ha-* appearing at the beginning of the verse or by a word indicating uncertainty, such as *mi* (who?), *mah* (what?), *lamah* (why?), etc. No interrogative marker appears in Job 2:9.

that has happened to you]." Job's wife is expressing wonder and appreciation. Indeed, God speaks these words about Job in the third person (using "he" instead of "you") in Job 2:3b: "He still is holding on to his integrity [despite all that has happened to him]" (translations mine). Aside from the pronouns, the phrases in Job 2:3b and 2:9a are the same.[36] However, the English makes it seem like Job's wife asks a question, whereas God utters a statement. This interrogative portrays her as a wife mocking her husband, instead of a woman understanding her partner's unwavering faith.

More startling is the rendering of *barekh* as the command "Curse!" in the second part of the verse instead of "Bless!" which is what *barekh* means.[37] If Job's wife admires her husband's enduring devotion ("You still are holding on to your integrity") and suggests that he seek God's favor and relief from his misery ("Bless God and die"), she appears as a compassionate spouse. But if she scorns her husband as foolish ("Do you still persist in your integrity?" [NRSV]) and blasphemes against God ("Curse God, and die" [NRSV]), Job's wife seems ill-tempered and unlikeable.

English Bibles often translate *barekh* as "curse" instead of "bless" even though the Hebrew conveys the latter.[38] Perhaps translators render *barekh* (bless) antiphrastically, or in its opposite sense, because of Job's reaction in the next verse, calling his wife one of the "foolish ones" (fem. plural form). In Job 1:11 and 2:5, forms of *barakh* appear in English as "curse" because this is the only

36. The Hebrew of Job 2:3 also adds the particle *vav*, meaning "and" at the beginning of the phrase, but otherwise the syntax is identical.

37. The Jewish prayer of thanks, *barukh attah adonai eloheinu melekh ha-olam*— "Blessed are you Lord our God king of the universe," begins with the same word (*barukh*, from *barekh*), with the meaning of blessing.

38. Most English translations render the first part of Job 2:9 as a question despite the lack of any interrogative particle. Along with the NRSV, the KJV and RSV translate the second part of the verse as, "Curse God, and die." The NIV adds an exclamation point, "Curse God and die!" and the ASV changes the verb: "Renounce God, and die." The NJPS keeps the first phrase as a statement: "You still keep your integrity!" then translates the second as "Blaspheme God, and die!" All these translations perpetuate negative understandings of Job's wife.

translation that makes sense. In both verses, *ha-satan* incites God to give over Job and explains that when Job loses his possessions or his health (respectively) he will "curse you to your face." The Hebrew word for "curse" in these two verses is a form of *barakh*.

A student of mine, Kim, once suggested in class that perhaps the pious scribes who wrote and copied biblical texts could not bear to see the word "curse" and references to God next to each other, so they used the word *barakh* ("bless") instead. Indeed, when the Hebrew Bible uses forms of *barakh* in a negative sense and the English translates the word as "curse," God is the object of the action.[39] Her point is well taken.

Yet the words *barakh* and God (*elohim*) together do not need to be translated only as "curse God." Usually forms of "bless" and "God" appear together in a positive sense (especially in the Psalms) and are rendered simply as "bless God."[40] In Job 1:21, the name of the Lord is "blessed" (*meborak*—a form of *barakh*). When Job's wife speaks, to translate *barakh* meaning either "curse" or "bless" would make sense, and both uses have precedence in the book of Job. So why do translators have Job's wife "cursing" instead of "blessing" God?

Without asking the translators of various English Bibles, we can only speculate about their intentions; nonetheless, we can assess the implications. As C. L. Seow explains regarding Job 2:9, "The word 'bless' . . . may be taken at face value or it may be understood as a euphemism, meaning 'curse.' Assuming the latter meaning, interpreters through the ages have roundly condemned Job's wife as an unthinking fool, an irritating nag, a heretic, a tempter, an unwitting tool of the devil, or even a personification of the devil

---

39. See also 1 Kings 21:10: "'You have cursed [*berakhta*] God and the king.' Then take him out, and stone him to death."

40. See Pss. 66:20; 68:26 [MT: 68:27]; also 72:18; 106:48. Forms of the words *barakh* and "the Lord" also appear together as an expression of reverence (Deut. 8:10; Judg. 5:2, 9; 1 Chron. 19:20; Neh. 9:5; Pss. 16:7; 34:1 [MT: 34:2]; 103:1, 2, 20, 21, 22; 104:1, 35; 134:1, 2; 135:19, 20).

himself."[41] When you catch that fleeting glance of Job's wife in 2:9, know that the Hebrew text portrays her more kindly than English translations. We can legitimately understand Job's wife as expressing awe for her husband's faithfulness ("You still are holding on to your integrity") and wishing him peace with his maker followed by the ultimate relief from his pain ("Bless God, and die."). With this reading, Job's harsh words in response to her kindness make *him* seem churlish and reactive, not her. Indeed, we can find in Job's wife another woman of the Bible to admire—a gracious, caring partner—who breaks through the silence imposed on her by the text to offer a word of love and mercy.

Women Musicians in the Ancient Near East (chap. 7)

Music was integral to life in the ancient Near East. In a world where every sound was live, music was not only a source of enjoyment and entertainment but also a way to honor deities, create community, celebrate victory, rouse troops, encourage work, lament defeat, proclaim greatness, facilitate childbirth, and express sorrow. Then, as now, music holds power not only for those who hear it but also for those who make it—including women.

The tradition of women as music-makers resonates loudly in ancient Egypt.[42] Veneration of the goddesses Hathor and Merit, who were both closely associated with music, contributed to the centrality of music in Egyptian culture. Some women served deities as music-making temple priestesses. More broadly, women, along with men, could develop lucrative careers as musicians.[43] The first professional singer recorded in Egyptian history was a woman named Iti, who rose to a position of great status in

41. Seow, "Job's Wife," 141. See also his commentary *Job 1–21*, 293–98.
42. For further discussion of women and music in ancient Egypt, see Graves-Brown, *Dancing for Hathor*, 90–97. On how roles of women as music-makers changed in ancient Egypt, see Gergis, "Power of Women Musicians."
43. Tyldesley, *Daughters of Isis*, 126.

Figure 10.1 Facsimile of a painting of Egyptian women musicians from the Tomb of Djeserkareseneb, ca. 1400–1390 BCE.

the mid-third millennium BCE (fifth dynasty).[44] Indeed, women were essential participants in the music that permeated Egyptian life.[45]

Evidence for women as music-makers in ancient Egypt can be seen in figure 10.1. Here women create music by playing an angular harp, a lute, a double flute, and a lyre (left to right) with a girl dancing in the middle. Similar scenes are relatively common in Egyptian iconography. Egyptologist Carolyn Graves-Brown points out that "women in general were associated with music."[46]

In ancient Mesopotamia, women also have a long and strong musical history, as attested in texts and ancient art. Mesopotamian civilization originated in Sumer, where women were musicians and singers. An elaborate limestone box inlaid with shells and lapis lazuli that dates from the mid-third millennium BCE, known as the Standard of Ur, depicts a man playing an

44. Gergis, "Power of Women Musicians," 189–90.
45. Strudwick, *Encyclopedia of Ancient Egypt*, 416–17.
46. Graves-Brown, *Dancing for Hathor*, 95.

Figure 10.2 Musicians depicted in the Standard of Ur Tomb 779, Royal Cemetery, Ur (modern Iraq), ca. 2600 BCE.

ornate lyre with a person behind him, apparently a singer (see fig. 10.2). This woman's hairstyle resembles that of Ur-Nanshe, a gender-ambiguous singer of Mari (in upper Mesopotamia) (see fig. 10.3).[47]

The later northern Mesopotamian empire of Neo-Assyria (912–612 BCE) offers further pictorial evidence of women as musicians through low-depth sculptures (bas-reliefs) carved into palace walls (see fig. 10.4).

The drawing depicted in figure 10.4 is based on a bas-relief from the palace of Nineveh (the capital of Assyria) showing a procession of people from the country of Elam (an ancient civilization from the region of modern Iran). Children clap while following the men and women playing lyres and double flutes, suggesting gender parity in instrumental use and ability.

In ancient Israel, women played the popular hand drum (*tof*; also translated as "frame drum") as stated in the Hebrew Bible

47. Stol, *Women in the Ancient Near East*, 354, 359.

and backed by archaeological evidence.[48] Biblical texts depict drums, dance, and song combining in performances of women and girls celebrating military victories (Exod. 15:20; Judg. 11:34; 1 Sam. 18:6–7).[49] In these verses, verbs that convey the actions of the drum players are in the feminine form. These passages offer images of female drum players that are corroborated by small terra-cotta statues of women playing drums (see fig. 10.5). Sarah Riley deduces that these figurines most commonly represent ordinary women making music or women with religious roles supplying music for rituals.[50] The Psalms repeatedly attest to hand drums being played in the temple (Pss. 68:24–25 [MT: 68:25–26]; 149:1, 3; 150:1, 4). Psalm 68:24–25 describes musicians entering the temple with teenage girls (*alamoth*) playing hand drums as part of this solemn procession. Carol Meyers proposes that girls and women rehearsed together for their performances.[51] The role of women and girls as hand drummers was part of the rhythm of ancient Israelite life.

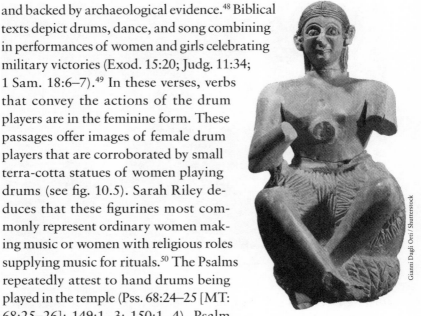

Gianni Dagli Orti / Shutterstock

Figure 10.3 A statue of Ur-Nanshe, from the Temple of Ishtar at Mari (modern Syria), ca. 2600–2500 BCE (displayed in the Syrian National Museum in Damascus).

In addition to drumming, further references to women as musicians emerge from settings of cultic activity.[52] Susan Ackerman examines the roles of girls dancing in the pilgrimage festival at

48. See Riley, "Hand Drum," 23. While *tof* is frequently rendered "tambourine," Carol Meyers notes that this translation is anachronistic, since bangles on the rims of drums were a much later addition. Meyers, "Women with Hand-Drums," 190.

49. Meyers, "Women with Hand-Drums," 190.

50. Riley, "Hand Drum," 26.

51. Meyers, "Of Drums and Damsels," 23–25.

52. See Marsman, *Women in Ugarit and Israel*, 552–55.

Figure 10.4 Illustration of a gypsum wall panel portraying Assyrian musicians, ca. 660–650 BCE (displayed in the British Museum). Originally drawn for the *Encycolpaedia Biblica* in 1903.

Figure 10.5 Terra-cotta figurines of young women playing hand drums, dating from around the eighth century BCE.

© 2014, Baker Publishing Group. Collection of the Israel Museum, Jerusalem, and courtesy of the Israel Antiquities Authority. Exhibited at the Israel Museum, Jerusalem.

Shiloh (Judg. 21:19–21).[53] Based on linguistic evidence, Ackerman suggests this scene transpires at the annual Ingathering/Sukkot festival in which girls play an integral role.[54] She ties this celebration in Shiloh to Hannah's song (1 Sam. 2:1–10) also taking place during the Sukkot festival.[55] Ackerman reveals further instances of women as cultic performers in Isaiah 5:1–7, Psalm 81:1–3 (MT: 81:2–4), and Jeremiah 31:10–14, as well as music-makers for life events such as funerary rites (Amos 5:16), mourning (Jer. 9:17–21 [MT: 9:16–20]), and rejoicing after military victories (Judg. 11:34; Ps. 68:11–12, 25–26 [MT: 68:12–13, 25–26]).[56]

53. While translators frequently refer to "young women" in Judg. 21:21, the Hebrew *venoth* (plural of *bat*) means "daughters" and often indicates girls before marriage (as here), which would have been early teenage years or younger.

54. Ackerman, *Women and the Religion of Ancient Israel*, 231–33.

55. Ackerman, *Women and the Religion of Ancient Israel*, 232–36.

56. Ackerman, *Women and the Religion of Ancient Israel*, 237–51.

Throughout the ancient Near East, women could be trained and accomplished musicians, known for their skills and valued for their talents. Women could also participate in making music in ways that did not require formal instruction but rather emerged from personal and communal needs. Once we attune ourselves to evidence from texts and iconography, the echoes of women's music in the ancient Near East reverberate through millennia to reach our ears.

Beyond the Binary (chap. 8)

Many people think the Bible sanctions only heterosexual, monogamous relationships between a cisgender man and a cisgender woman, but that understanding (like any other) stems from the interpreter's own biases. Biblical texts can also support people who are queer, transgender, and nonbinary.[57]

Sexual and gender diversity are part of God's creation, as seen in the Bible's opening chapter where God creates the world in seven days (Gen. 1:1–2:4a). Day one brings light and dark, forming evening and morning (1:3–5); day two: the dome of the sky (vv. 6–8); day three: seas and earth with vegetation (vv. 9–13); day four: the sun, moon, and stars (vv. 14–19); day five: creatures of the air (birds) and seas (fish) (vv. 20–23); day six: land animals (vv. 24–25) and finally—male and female humans (vv. 26–30). (After all this divine work, God [understandably] rests [2:1–4a].) But a lot is missing. Does midday exist? Are there no planets? What about lakes and rivers, if all the water has been "gathered together into one place" (1:9)? Where are the amphibious creatures? Instead of listing

---

57. A cisgender person is someone whose gender identity matches their sex assigned at birth. A transgender person is someone whose gender identity is different from their sex assigned at birth. Nonbinary people are those whose gender identity is not male or female. Heterosexual people are attracted to the opposite sex. Those who identify as queer may be attracted to the same sex (homosexual), both sexes (bisexual), neither sex (asexual), or all sexual identities (pansexual). For further terminology, see "Glossary of Terms," the Human Rights Campaign, https://www.hrc.org/resources/glossary-of-terms.

everything in the universe, two contrasting elements (day/night; sun/moon; seas/land; birds/fish, etc.) encompass all in-between. This literary device is called a merism, and the Bible employs it repeatedly.[58]

Accordingly, the creation of male and female humans does not limit sexuality to heterosexuality or gender expressions to either binary. Just as the polarities of evening and morning contain midday, the spectrum ends of male and female incorporate transgender, intersex, and nonbinary people. God underscores this inclusivity in proclaiming, "Let us make humankind [Hebrew: *adam*] in *our* image, according to *our* likeness" (Gen. 1:26a). Why does God speak in the plural? Perhaps the omniscient Creator not only recognizes but affirms that human sexuality and gender identities come in many forms, all of which are encompassed in God. In Genesis 1:26b, God entrusts people to take care of the earth's creatures. When the text reverts to the male/female language of Genesis 1:27, it has already established these terms as the wide extensions of the gender merism. Then God pronounces that the entire creation—including the people who come in a broad range of identities, all of which are in God's own image—is not only good but "very good" (v. 31).

Along with other biblical texts, Genesis 1 has been interpreted to promote heterosexism that not only allows but encourages discrimination.[59] Indeed, verses cited to demean anyone who is not heteronormative are known as "clobber" passages, taken out of context to beat people down.[60] Is that how we want to use the Bible?

---

58. For example, the Israelites' longing for the land flowing with "milk and honey" (Exod. 3:8, 17; 13:5; 33:3; Lev. 20:24; Num. 13:27; 14:8; 16:13, 14, to cite a few of many attestations) can be understood to indicate all foods, ranging from those that spoil quickly (milk) to those that never spoil (honey). The Psalmist's affirmation that God knows "when I sit down and when I rise up" (Ps. 139:2) suggests all activities, not just these two. God's claiming the role of "the Alpha and the Omega" (Rev. 1:8; 21:6; 22:13) does not indicate the first and last letters of the Greek alphabet but, rather, refers to all-encompassing worldly power.

59. For documentation and theological discussion, see Hornsby's introduction in Hornsby and Guest's *Transgender, Intersex, and Biblical Interpretation*. On modern binary gender divisions and biblical texts, see Tamber-Rosenau, "Queer Critique," 484–91.

60. For analysis of weaponized biblical texts, see Martin, *UnClobber*; see also Vines, *God and the Gay Christian*.

Conversely, we can celebrate biblical texts that reflect the values we seek to emulate—love, generosity, courage, compassion—in all kinds of people and relationships. With this lens, we perceive that David and Jonathan were two men who found their love wonderful, "passing the love of women" (2 Sam. 1:26).[61] Ruth and Naomi's story ends portraying two women and their child, with Boaz as the sperm donor (Ruth 4:13–17).[62] Jesus brings dead Lazarus back to life by calling him to "Come out!" from the tomb so the community can "unbind him and let him go" (John 11:43–44). For many queer people, this biblical story can be a powerful metaphor for coming out of the closet.[63]

Biblical characters who are clearly outside of the gender binary are acclaimed as the heroes of their stories. A eunuch, Ebed-melech, approaches the king about Jeremiah's dire plight after the prophet has been placed in a muddy cistern, and indeed Ebed-melech rescues him (Jer. 38:6–13). In the New Testament, the Ethiopian eunuch, a royal official, offers a model of intelligence and faith as he questions Scripture, seeks understanding, and is baptized by Philip (Acts 8:26–38).[64] Acts 8:32–33 specifies that the Ethiopian eunuch is pondering a section of Isaiah's prophecy, known to us as Isaiah 53:7–8, an excerpt from one of the "suffering servant" passages.[65] Perhaps the eunuch read further to the text we know as Isaiah 56:3–5, 8, in which God's affirmation of a nonbinary person and all who are made to feel outcast is profound.[66]

61. See Stone, "1 and 2 Samuel," 205–8.

62. This interpretation is from Travis, "Love Your Mother," 38–39; see also Duncan, "Book of Ruth."

63. See Perkins, "Coming Out, Lazarus's and Ours."

64. On the role of eunuchs, especially in the New Testament, see Knust, *Unprotected Texts*, 68–69; see also Marchal, "LGBTIQ Strategies of Interpretation."

65. Isaiah 42:1–4; 49:1–6; 50:4–11; and 52:13–53:12 refer to a figure whom scholars call the "suffering servant," whose obedience to God includes enduring pain and death for the sins of others.

66. I am grateful to Eric Thomas for sharing this imaginative possibility with me.

Do not let the foreigner joined to the LORD say,
    "The LORD will surely separate me from his people";
and do not let the eunuch say,
    "I am just a dry tree."
For thus says the LORD:
To the eunuchs who keep my sabbaths,
    who choose the things that please me
    and hold fast my covenant,
I will give, in my house and within my walls,
    a monument and a name
    better than sons and daughters;
I will give them an everlasting name
    that shall not be cut off. . . .

Thus says the LORD GOD,
    who gathers the outcasts of Israel,
I will gather others to them
    besides those already gathered. (Isa. 56:3–5, 8)

The Bible affirms that *all* people are equally formed in God's image; therefore, *all* people deserve equality. Justice is not a pie: if someone gets more someone else gets less. If queer, transgender, and nonbinary people have rights, cisgendered heterosexual people do not have fewer rights. Rather, human rights are strengthened for everyone. In this kind of world, the one God originally created, every body lives—safely and joyfully—into the fullest expression of their God-imaged self.

Martha, or More Mary? (chap. 9)

This final section consists of an interview with Elizabeth Schrader Polczer, a Bible scholar whose research has been getting a lot of well-merited attention.[67] I first met Elizabeth when she gave

---

67. Elizabeth Schrader Polczer (PhD, Duke University) is assistant professor of New Testament at Villanova University. Some articles highlighting her scholarship

a lecture at General Theological Seminary in New York City, a school where I have taught and where Elizabeth earned a master's degree (before I joined the faculty). In this talk, she explained her theory that Martha was editorially added to some of our earliest handwritten copies of John 11, the story of Lazarus being raised from the tomb. She showed slide after slide of ancient Greek manuscripts in which the name Mary was changed to Martha and the reference to one sister of Lazarus changed to two sisters. What does this mean? How did she discover these textual alterations, and why do they matter? Elizabeth graciously met with me to explain more about her scholarship so I could share it with you.

> ME: The story of how you became a Bible scholar is fascinating. Would you say a little about that journey, please?
>
> ELIZABETH: Sure. I was a singer/songwriter living in Brooklyn.[68] I wrote a song on Mary Magdalene and then felt strangely compelled to learn more about her. Through the Episcopal priest of my home church in Portland, Oregon, I found out about Dr. Deirdre Good, a New Testament professor who was teaching at General and has done extensive research on Mary Magdalene. We both were living in New York City, so I met her for coffee. Little did I know how this encounter would set me on a path that changed my life.
>
> ME: What happened?
>
> ELIZABETH: I told Dr. Good that I wanted to investigate the oldest complete copy of John's Gospel, Papyrus 66 [which dates from approximately 200 CE], and she informed me that it was digitally available online. When I looked at this

---

include Moss, "Conspiracy to Suppress Mary Magdalene?"; Shimron, "Scribes Tried to Blot Her Out"; and Shimron, "Was Mary Magdalene Really from Magdala?"

68. To hear some of Elizabeth's songs, including the one on Mary Magdalene, go to ElizabethSchrader.com and click on the music tab. The song is titled "Magdalene."

manuscript, I saw that the name Mary had been crossed out twice in a row in the first five verses of John 11! At this point, I didn't know Greek, so I used an interlinear Bible to see what each word meant. Even as a layperson, I could see that Martha's presence was unstable. The scribe was changing letters to add in her name—I was astounded![69] I sent this information to Dr. Good, who probably assumed that work had already been done on this significant textual discrepancy because Papyrus 66 had been discovered over fifty years prior. But I couldn't shake the feeling that something surprising was going on with this biblical story. I went to the Brooklyn Public Library and read all I could. I contacted well-known scholars and called the textual changes to their attention, but they were busy, and I think they also felt this work must have already been done. Finally, my best friend told me that I needed to stop bothering scholars and start learning Greek. I said, "Noooooo—that sounds horrible!" For a year, I dillydallied. But the following fall I started a master's degree.

ME: How did your studies progress?

ELIZABETH: I made textual criticism [the scholarship of examining early manuscripts] of John 11 the focus of my master's thesis. With the seminary's databases, I was able to explore not only more Greek manuscripts but also the tradition of Old Latin manuscripts and the work of the church fathers.[70] I found repeated evidence from early Christian traditions that suggested Lazarus had only one sister: Mary. Not only

---

69. In Greek, the change from the name Mary (*maria*) to Martha (*martha*) requires only one letter substitution, with the second to last letter altered from an *iota* to a *theta*. In John 11:1, with proper nouns in the genitive case, this change is from Μαρίας to Μάρθας.

70. Early Latin manuscripts are handwritten copies of biblical texts dating from the first centuries CE, prior to Jerome's Latin translation of the Vulgate in the late fourth to early fifth centuries. The "early church fathers" refers to Christian theologians who wrote from the late first to mid-eighth centuries and created foundational Christian doctrines.

was the name Mary changed to Martha in several crucial manuscripts of John 11, but I also encountered manuscripts where the reference to one sister (Mary) was changed to two (Mary and Martha). These scribal alterations were not in most manuscripts, but nonetheless I repeatedly saw the same discrepancies throughout the Lazarus episode. When the thesis was done, I told Dr. Good that I wanted to see if the *Harvard Theological Review* would publish it. I chose that journal because I knew this research was important. But when they accepted my thesis to publish as an article, I was so surprised![71]

ME: I'm not surprised at all. I read the article, and you mount a persuasive scholarly argument. You give the thesis and then lay out the evidence.

ELIZABETH: And there is a lot of evidence!

ME: So what are the implications of Martha being added to the story of Lazarus being raised from the tomb?

ELIZABETH: Well, we need to be cautious because even though Martha is blinking in and out, she still appears in all manuscripts of John 11, so we do not have definitive proof of my theory. But I think it is possible that in the earliest circulating version of John's Gospel, instead of Lazarus having two sisters, he just had one, named Mary. And she may have been Mary Magdalene.

ME: Why do you think Lazarus's sister, Mary, and Mary Magdalene could be the same person? Wasn't Mary a common name?

ELIZABETH: Yes, it definitely was, but the evangelist who wrote John's Gospel repeatedly connects Mary with Lazarus in John 11 to Mary Magdalene with Jesus in John 20. Both scenes portray a woman at a tomb (11:17–20, 31; 20:1), she's

---

71. Schrader, "Was Martha of Bethany Added to the Fourth Gospel?"

crying (11:33; 20:11), there's a stone that is moved (11:38–39, 41; 20:1), and a handkerchief (which is an unusual detail) (11:44; 20:7).[72] And the same question appears: "Where have you laid him?" (11:34; 20:13, 15). In our Bibles now, a minor character, Martha, proclaims Jesus as the Christ (11:27). But I think John may have intended to portray Mary Magdalene as the woman making this profound Christological confession.

ME: Then why wouldn't John just say that Mary Magdalene proclaimed Jesus as the Messiah?

ELIZABETH: Giving her this elevated status may have been too controversial. Peter gives the same confession of faith in Matthew's Gospel (Matt. 16:16). We have multiple early Christian writings of Peter complaining about Mary Magdalene's prominence among Jesus' followers.[73] I think John was aware of this tension. The deliberate crafting of similarities between these two tomb scenes sends the reader persistent clues that Lazarus's sister is Mary Magdalene, instead of directly making an assertion that might have caused John's Gospel to be rejected.

ME: So Mary Magdalene would then be a very prominent and powerful leader in the earliest Christian communities, is that right?

ELIZABETH: It's certainly possible.

ME: Your proposal puts forth a major change in how we think about Mary Magdalene. And your text-critical argument is very compelling.

ELIZABETH: Thank you so much!

---

72. The same Greek word, *soudariō*, in John 11:44 and 20:7 is generally translated as "cloth" but is defined more accurately as "handkerchief."

73. For example, the Gospel of Mary, an early Christian text from the mid-second century, gives an account of the resurrected Jesus and the first apostles. Peter and Andrew challenge Mary's authority as a woman who received a vision from Christ. For further discussion, see King, *Gospel of Mary of Magdala*, 83–92.

ME: It amazes me to think that your song "Magdalene" started you on the path to becoming a Bible scholar. In your song, which I love, by the way [Elizabeth: I'm glad.], you sing about "the long-hidden knowledge of the Magdalene." It seems like you are uncovering that knowledge with these manuscript discoveries that shift our thinking around Mary Magdalene. I feel that new ways of reading and interpreting biblical texts really can upend our assumptions, and even alter our self-perceptions and ways of being in the world.

ELIZABETH: Studying women of the Bible has certainly changed my life.

ME: Mine too!

Appendix 1

Bible Basics

I found the Bible confusing until I studied it in seminary, even though I grew up in a religious home. My Sunday school teachers (God bless them) taught me biblical stories, so as a child I could tell you about Moses, Jesus, Jonah, David, and Mary, and maybe a few other Bible luminaries. But I didn't know how different characters or episodes related to each other, if at all. Many books of the Bible (Ecclesiastes? Judges? Hebrews?) remained a mystery. And because I was the daughter of a minister, my lack of biblical knowledge felt, at points, embarrassing.

While trying to make sense of the Bible, I needed a framework for understanding. If you—smart, curious reader—also feel challenged in making sense of the Bible, you are not alone. The Bible is not easy literature. Yet acquiring knowledge about the Bible is well worth the effort because of this book's powerful cultural presence. And for me, and perhaps you too, the Bible is also a cherished spiritual treasure. When I found the Bible so bewildering, I wish I had had a really simple guide like the one that follows.

Even speaking of "the Bible" is tricky, since faith traditions vary in the books they hold sacred. Here I briefly sketch the differences among Jewish, Catholic, Orthodox, and Protestant Bibles, then follow Protestant order and include books in the Catholic Apocrypha. Answering basic questions—Who? What? Where? When? Why? How?—provides a scaffold for biblical knowledge.

So here you go, my reader friend.

With one catch.

If you know any Bible scholars, please do not show them the following summary. (*Let it be our little secret.*) Trust me, your academic friend is all too apt to look at the chart below with a roll of the eyes—it's too simple! The Bible is intellectually rich and culturally complex! True and truer. But sometimes a plain road map offers a straightforward way to begin exploration and is better than no guidance at all.

A Simple, Friendly Overview of a Complicated Book

Who?

Who wrote the Bible?

Lots of people wrote the Old Testament. Most of the authors are unknown. Some prophets (and a few others, like Ezra and Nehemiah) may have written the books that bear their names, but we do not have evidence for these claims beyond the Bible itself.

A smaller number of people wrote the New Testament. Most of the authors are anonymous. We call the Gospel writers "Matthew," "Mark," "Luke," and "John," but it is hard to know for sure who wrote these texts. The apostle Paul wrote some of the formal letters (called Epistles) credited to him, although scholars disagree on how many.

What?

What is the Bible?

The word "bible" means "books" (from the Greek *biblia*). That's it. The Bible is a collection of books that Christian and Jewish traditions hold sacred.

What does the Bible consist of?

Jews call their Bible the *Tanakh* (which is an acronym from the Hebrew words: *Torah*, *Nevi'im*, and *Ketuvim*). The Jewish Bible consists of twenty-four books that focus on the ancient people of Israel and their relationship with God. The same material is found in the Old Testament's thirty-nine books, arranged differently.

The first five books together are called the *Torah* (Hebrew for "instruction"). The second part is called *Nevi'im* (Hebrew for "prophets"). The third part is called the *Ketuvim* (Hebrew for "writings").

The Christian Bible consists of the Old Testament and the New Testament combined.

The Old Testament (sometimes called the First Testament) is another presentation of the books of the Hebrew Scriptures (or *Tanakh*). It was written before Jesus was born.

Some Christian traditions include more books in their Bibles, before the New Testament. The Protestant Old Testament has thirty-nine books. The Old Testament of the Roman Catholic Bible has forty-six books (plus longer versions of two books—Esther and Daniel). The Old Testament of the Orthodox Bible has fifty books (plus an extra Psalm).

So if you ever find yourself in a pay-one-price Bible store—go for the Orthodox version—it's the best value!

The New Testament (sometimes called the Second Testament) consists of twenty-seven books that focus on Jesus and early Christian communities. It was written not long after Jesus died and contains the same books in the same order in all Christian traditions.

What are the languages of the Bible?

The Old Testament (or *Tanakh*) was written in Hebrew, with a few chapters and verses in Aramaic (a language similar to Hebrew and using the same alphabet). The New Testament was written in Greek.

Where?

Where was the Bible written?

A lot of the Old Testament was likely written or edited in Babylon (in modern-day Iraq). Portions were also written in the land now known as Israel/Palestine and its environs. The New Testament was written in the area around the eastern part of the Mediterranean Sea, including modern-day Israel/Palestine, Syria, Greece, and Turkey.

Where do the stories of the Bible take place?

The land of the Old Testament is usually called the ancient Near East and is largely centered in the modern Middle East. Most of the stories relate to the lands of modern Israel/Palestine, Egypt, Jordan, Lebanon, Syria, Iraq, and Iran.

The stories and letters of the New Testament are centered in the areas where they were written: modern-day Israel/Palestine, Syria, Greece, Turkey, extending as far west as Rome.

When?

When was the Bible written?

The Old Testament was written between 1200 and 167 (approximately) BCE (or BC).[1] The New Testament was written between 50 and 120 (approximately) CE (or AD). Many of the Bible's stories likely circulated orally before being written down.

When do the stories of the Bible take place?

The biblical story starts with the creation of the world, then focuses on Abraham and Sarah's lineage leading to the Israelite people, beginning around 1800 BCE. The Old Testament's story ends with the rebuilding of the Jerusalem temple, in the fourth century BCE (even though some texts were written later and set earlier).

---

1. Since evidence is ancient and limited, it is hard to know precisely when texts were written and dates remain a source of scholarly debate.

The New Testament starts with Jesus' birth, around the year 0. Most of its stories are set in the first century and the first part of the second century CE. Its story ends with the final judgment of the world and a new heaven and new earth.

Why?

Why did people write the books that became our Bible?
The writers of the Old Testament wanted people to believe in and follow one particular God, whose name was known by four Hebrew letters: יהוה, transliterated as Yhwh and translated as "the Lord." Various kinds of literature explore the people's history and relationship with God.

The writers of the New Testament wanted people to believe that Jesus of Nazareth was the Christ (or the Messiah), which means "Anointed" (by God).

How?

How did people write the Bible?
The Bible was written on parchment, which is treated animal skin (like leather), or papyrus, which was made from the plant of the same name. Ink came from natural sources, usually a combination of charcoal, gum, and water.

Only a small percentage of people in antiquity knew how to read or write. Those who were literate generally came from the upper classes because they could afford to spend their time getting a formal education.

How can I know what is in the Bible?
Again, the Bible is very complex—but below, intelligent, curious reader, is a rough idea of what you will find in each book of the Bible.

Books of the Old Testament (also called the *Hebrew Bible* or the *Tanakh*)

Torah or Pentateuch

The first five books are foundational for the rest of the Bible. They tell about the origins of the world (in Genesis) and the beginnings of the Israelite people.

Book name	Key themes	Key characters (add God to nearly every list)
Genesis	beginning of the world	Adam, Eve, Noah
	beginnings of the Israelite people	Abraham, Sarah, Hagar, Ishmael, Isaac, Rebekah, Jacob, Leah, Rachel, Joseph and brothers
Exodus	enslaved Israelites leave Egypt freed Israelites wander in the wilderness Moses gives laws and guidelines	Moses, Pharaoh, Miriam, Aaron, Israelites
Leviticus	guidelines for daily and cultic life	Moses, Aaron, priests, Israelites
Numbers	struggles in the wilderness	Moses, Aaron, Joshua, Israelites
Deuteronomy	getting ready for life in the promised land	Moses, Israelites

The Historical Books

The historical books tell the story of the Israelites invading Canaan then establishing themselves in their new promised land, forming their own monarchy, the splitting apart of that monarchy into northern and southern kingdoms, and the conquering of those kingdoms by empires from Mesopotamia.[2] The people

2. The books of the Bible that are in two parts—Samuel, Kings, and Chronicles—were each originally one book (e.g., Samuel instead of 1 Samuel and 2 Samuel). Since these books are so long, it was hard to fit all the words on one scroll. Taken together, the books of Joshua, Judges, 1 and 2 Samuel, and 1 and 2 Kings form what scholars call the Deuteronomistic History. Ruth is set in the "time of the judges" but probably was written after the other books.

of Jerusalem are exiled to Babylon, where they remain for about fifty years. When Persia conquers Babylon and King Cyrus allows the Jews to return home, many go back to Jerusalem to rebuild the temple.

Book name	Key themes	Key characters (add God to nearly every list)
Joshua	conquering the land of the Canaanites	Joshua, Caleb, Israelites
Judges	various tribal leaders help the Israelites as they settle in the promised land	Deborah, Gideon, Jephthah, Samson, and other judges with the Israelite tribes
Ruth	a short story set in the time of the judges about a family trying to survive after a famine	Ruth, Naomi, Boaz
1 Samuel	tribes unite and Israel forms a kingdom Saul becomes Israel's first king	Samuel, Saul, David, Israelites
2 Samuel	the reign of David as Israel's great king (and his flaws)	David and his entourage of prophets, advisers, soldiers, wives, and children
1 Kings	Solomon (David's son) as the last king of the united monarchy and its division into two parts: the north (Israel) and the south (Judah)	Solomon, Elijah, Ahab, Jezebel, Rehoboam, Jeroboam
2 Kings	rulers of both kingdoms and the fall of Israel to Assyria and Judah to Babylon people of Jerusalem are exiled to Babylon (for a period of about fifty years, called the exile)	kings of Judah and Israel, Elisha, rulers of the Assyrians and Babylonians
1 Chronicles	genealogies, history of Israel and Judah from a pro-David perspective	early figures in genealogies, David and his officials
2 Chronicles	history from Solomon to the return to the land after the exile, mostly focused on Judah	Solomon, subsequent kings of Judah

Book name	Key themes	Key characters (add God to nearly every list)
Ezra	exiles return to Judah after living in Babylon for two generations	Ezra (a priest and scribe), the returned exiles
Nehemiah	returned exiles rebuild the walls of Jerusalem	Nehemiah (a governor), the returned exiles
Esther	a story about Jews living in Persia and the queen who saves them	Esther, Mordecai, King Ahasuerus, Haman

The Poetic and Wisdom Books

These writings probe the questions and challenges of everyday life and focus more on the individual than on peoples, rulers, prophets, or nations.

Book name	Key themes	Key characters (add God to nearly every list)
Job	Why do good people suffer?	God, the Adversary, Job, Job's friends
Psalms	a collection of songs expressing heartfelt feelings and reaching out to God	no specified characters—just those who offer the song-prayers (the psalmists)
Proverbs	a collection of sayings to guide one through life	Woman Wisdom, the Strange Woman, the voices of the advice-givers
Ecclesiastes	one person's insights about the meaning of life	Qoheleth (designation for the person whose thoughts fill the book)
Song of Songs	erotic love poetry	a woman and man sharing their passionate desire for each other

The Prophetic Books

A prophet is someone who acts as an intermediary between God and the people. Common themes in the prophetic books are social justice, obedience to God's covenant, rewards for being faithful, and punishments for being disloyal to God.

Isaiah, Jeremiah, and Ezekiel are called "major" prophets because their books are longer than the others.

Book name	Key themes	Key characters (add God to nearly every list)
Isaiah	judgment, restoration, and comfort God's power in times of crisis	Isaiah, Hezekiah (king of Judah), Cyrus (king of Persia)
Jeremiah	no worship of other gods turning to God in the face of enemy aggression	Jeremiah, Baruch (a scribe), Nebuchadnezzar (king of Babylon)
Lamentations[a]	lament over the destruction of Jerusalem	suffering people of destroyed Jerusalem
Ezekiel	dramatic visions of the prophet/priest living among the exiles concern for ritual purity	Ezekiel, Jerusalem inhabitants exiled to Babylon
Daniel[b]	living as an exile and keeping faith	Daniel, exiles in Babylon, Nebuchadnezzar

a. Lamentations is grouped with the prophetic books because early interpretative tradition held that Jeremiah wrote Lamentations.

b. Daniel is not like the other prophetic books since the first half is filled with stories (not words of prophecy). However, the book of Daniel is set in Babylon so it comes right after Ezekiel.

The "minor" prophets (with shorter books) are Hosea, Joel, Amos, Obadiah, Jonah, Micah, Nahum, Habakkuk, Zephaniah, Haggai, Zechariah, Malachi.

These twelve prophetic books are sometimes called "The Book of the Scroll" because their combined words could fit on one scroll. The text usually focuses on the words of these prophets and does not provide a lot of information about their lives.

Book name	Key themes	Key characters (add God to nearly every list)
Hosea	worship God alone, not Baal	Hosea, Gomer, Israelites who hear prophecy
Joel	repent beware of destruction	Joel, people of Zion (Jerusalem) who hear prophecy

Book name	Key themes	Key characters (add God to nearly every list)
Amos	anger at the rich spurn hollow worship	Amos, Israelites who hear prophecy
Obadiah	prophecy against the nation of Edom	Obadiah, doomed people of Edom
Jonah	a story about a reluctant and successful prophet	Jonah, a big fish, people and animals of Nineveh
Micah	punishment for oppression repent and have hope	Micah, people of Samaria and Jerusalem
Nahum	prophecy against the city of Nineveh	Nahum, doomed people of Nineveh
Habakkuk	questioning God concern for justice appeal for mercy	Habakkuk, oppressors and oppressed
Zephaniah	divine warrior brings judgment and eventual restoration	Zephaniah, people of Judah and their enemies
Haggai	rebuild the temple that was destroyed	Haggai, Zerubbabel (the governor), Joshua (the high priest)
Zechariah	visions purification restoration chastisement of other nations	Zechariah, Zerubbabel (the governor), Joshua (the high priest)
Malachi	accusations against people and priests judgment and mercy	Malachi, priests, evildoers, righteous ones

Apocrypha (also called Deuterocanonical Books)

The word "apocrypha" means "hidden things," but there is nothing hidden about these books. They were written in Hebrew, Greek, and Aramaic between the third century BCE and the first century CE.

Roman Catholic, Greek Orthodox, and Slavonic traditions hold the following books as sacred.[3]

Book name	Key themes	Key characters (add God to nearly every list)
Tobit	piety and survival under foreign rule	Tobit, Tobias, Sarah, Raphael (an angel)
Judith	strength cunning murder piety	Judith, Jews, Holofernes, Assyrians
Wisdom of Solomon	Greek philosophy Jewish pride	speech by "Solomon" to other kings
Ecclesiasticus *also called* **Wisdom of Jesus Son of Sirach**	proverbs, hymns, prayers, and blessings	Jesus (not Jesus of Nazareth) giving counsel
Baruch	sin exile repentance wisdom consolation	"Baruch" (scribe of Jeremiah)
Sometimes included		
Letter of Jeremiah	against worship of idols	"Jeremiah" to Babylonian exiles
1 Maccabees	resisting Greek domination Maccabean revolt	Judas Maccabeus, Antiochus IV
2 Maccabees	Maccabean revolt (more pious account than 1 Macc.)	Judas Maccabeus, Antiochus IV, Jewish mother and sons who refuse pork; sons tortured to death
Additions to Esther	piety and prayers added to Esther	Esther, Mordecai

3. Further books included (not as widely) in the Apocrypha are 1 Esdras, 2 Esdras, 3 Esdras, Prayer of Manasseh, Psalm 151, and 3 Maccabees in Greek and Slavonic Bibles; 2 Esdras and 4 Esdras in the Slavonic Bible and Latin Vulgate appendix; and 4 Maccabees in an appendix to the Greek Bible.

Book name	Key themes	Key characters (add God to nearly every list)
Additions to Daniel *(includes the following three books)*		
Prayer of Azariah and the Song of the Three Jews	hymns prayers of men in fiery furnace	Azariah, Hananiah, Mishael (Dan. 3)
Susanna	virtue integrity entrapment justice	Susanna, two lecherous elders, Daniel
Bel and the Dragon	faithfulness to and from God	Bel (an idol), deceptive priestly families, a dragon (falsely worshiped), Daniel, lions, the prophet Habakkuk

Books of the New Testament

Gospels

The first four books of the New Testament recount Jesus' life, mostly focusing on his ministry, betrayal, suffering, death, and resurrection.

Book name	Key themes	Key characters (God's presence is assumed in every book)
Matthew **Mark** **Luke**	The first three Gospels (Matthew, Mark, and Luke) are called the Synoptic Gospels.[a] They give similar stories about Jesus' ministry, death, and resurrection. Jesus is portrayed as the Messiah (or Christ) even though he was not a mighty king.	In addition to Jesus, other key characters are Mary (Jesus' mother), John the Baptist, Pontius Pilate, Mary Magdalene, Peter, Judas, and the other disciples (or close followers of Jesus).
John	John's Gospel contains some of the same stories as the Synoptic Gospels, but it places a stronger emphasis on Jesus as God's son.	John's Gospel contains most of the same characters as the Synoptic Gospels.

a. "Synoptic" means "seen together."

Acts of the Apostles

Acts provides a sequel to Luke's Gospel, written by the same author, to show how Jesus' ministry continues after his death and resurrection. Much of the book focuses on Paul, an early apostle.

Book name	Key themes	Key characters (God's presence is assumed in every book)
Acts	spreading belief in Jesus forming Christian communities	Peter, Paul, Philip, and various apostles (those who are sent out to promote belief in Jesus as the Christ)

Epistles

Epistles are stylized letters. Most of these letters claim to be written by the apostle Paul, but many scholars think that some epistles were written by later believers in Jesus (below listed as "Paul"). The letters often address situations in specific early communities of faith and appear in order of longest to shortest.

Book name	Key themes	Key characters (God's presence is assumed in every book)
Romans	salvation for all people	Paul to early Christ believers in Rome (including prominent women)
1 Corinthians	advice for community problems	Paul to early Christ believers in Corinth
2 Corinthians	subsequent letter to the same group of believers following up on community matters	Paul to early Christ believers in Corinth
Galatians	relationship between law and faith all people (circumcised or not) can be Christ believers	Paul to early Christ believers in Galatia
Ephesians	written from prison gentiles and Jews should live in harmony	"Paul" to early Christ believers in Ephesus

Book name	Key themes	Key characters (God's presence is assumed in every book)
Philippians	written from prison encourages new believers	Paul to early Christ believers in Philippi
Colossians	written from prison promotes divinity of Christ	"Paul" to early Christ believers in Colossae
1 Thessalonians	earliest letter (and Christian document) addresses end-of-the-world expectations	Paul to pagan converts in Thessalonica
2 Thessalonians	encouragement for those suffering persecution and visions of the end of the world	"Paul" to believers expecting Christ's imminent return
1 Timothy	problems with leadership in the church	"Paul" to Timothy (a young friend and colleague)
2 Timothy	urges expulsion of false teachers	"Paul" to Timothy (same friend)
Titus	leadership qualifications and moral instruction	"Paul" to Titus (a friend and colleague)
Philemon	written from prison advocates for a slave	Paul to Philemon (slave owner), Onesimus (the slave)

General Epistles

The General Epistles exhibit some features of Epistles but likely were not written from one individual to a specific recipient or community. The writers profess to be among Jesus' first apostles, but scholars doubt these claims due to writing style, concerns expressed, and chronology.

Book name	Key themes	Key characters (God's presence is assumed in every book)
Hebrews	sermon on the power of Christ (not technically an epistle)	"Paul" to Christians familiar with Judaism
James	faith shown by speech, generosity, and care for those in need	"James" to early believers
1 Peter	stay together amid persecution	"Peter" to Christians in Asia Minor

Book name	Key themes	Key characters (God's presence is assumed in every book)
2 Peter	false teachers coming of Christ final judgment	"Peter" to second-century Christians
1 John	true believers versus anti-christs hope in Jesus	"John" to Christ believers
2 John	love one another be wary of deceitful people	from "the elder" to "the elect lady and her children"
3 John	walk in truth imitate good	from "the elder" to Gaius
Jude	warning against false teachers exhortation to faithfulness	"Jude" (Jesus' brother) to Christ believers

Apocalyptic Literature

Revelation tells of the end of the world through a series of fantastical visions.

Book name	Key themes	Key characters
Revelation	visions of the end of the world and a new Jerusalem	enthroned God, Jesus as a lamb, strange creatures, Satan

The Bible starts with the beginning of the world and concludes with the end of the world. In between, it offers its own world of faith, hardship, joy, worship, hope, and awe.

Appendix 2

Resources for Further Exploration

In addition to the works cited in the bibliography, I would like to offer a few detailed suggestions of books you might find interesting. Below please find a select annotated list of resources that are helpful if you remain curious (like Eve!) and would like to increase your knowledge of the Bible and feminist biblical interpretation.

Barr, Beth Allison. *The Making of Biblical Womanhood: How the Subjugation of Women Became Gospel Truth*. Grand Rapids: Brazos, 2021.

This book is written by a medieval historian who traces and questions the development of ideas about the inferior roles of women as integral to Christianity. Dr. Barr's experiences in her evangelical tradition reveal the subjugation many Christian women are taught to embrace. Convincing research and personal testimony call out and challenge the damage some churches can do to women, stemming from patriarchal inter-pretations of biblical texts.

Dube, Musa W. *Postcolonial Feminist Interpretation of the Bible*. St. Louis: Chalice, 2000.

Written by an African New Testament scholar, this book reveals how Western ways of interpreting the Bible can be oppres-sive and harmful when imposed on other places in the world. Dr. Dube calls attention to abuse of the Bible as a tool of impe-rialism and exploitation. She then offers decolonializing reading strategies and applies them to Matthew 15:21–28, offering an interpretation attentive to women in the majority world.

Gafney, Wilda C. *Womanist Midrash: A Reintroduction to the Women of the Torah and the Throne*. Louisville: Westminster John Knox, 2017.

Wilda Gafney brings a womanist lens to academic and trans-lational analysis of Hebrew Bible texts focused on women and girls. (Womanist scholarship is feminist scholarship from black women or women of color who rightfully call white feminists to accountability for privileged assumptions.) Filling in gaps of the text (the tradition of midrash), Dr. Gafney includes short, creative essays to flesh out the characters' stories. Portraits of well-known and not-so-well-known female characters from the Hebrew Bible come together in this creative academic resource.

Hylen, Susan E. *Women in the New Testament World*. Oxford: Oxford University Press, 2019.

This book examines the contradictions surrounding women in the New Testament world. Women were expected to be subservient in Greco-Roman culture yet had active roles of leadership in households and in early Christian communities. Dr. Hylen examines these tensions by looking at expectations around women's virtues, marital status, class, occupations, and speech. Her discussion highlights the complexity of the place of women in the New Testament world and cautions against facile assumptions.

Mayfield, Tyler D. *A Guide to Bible Basics*. Louisville: Westminster John Knox, 2018.

Unlike the other books on this list, this one is not feminist or womanist but rather a general overview to understanding the Bible. If the short glimpse at each Bible book in appendix 1 leaves you wanting more straightforward information, you will find Dr. Mayfield's volume very helpful. Every biblical book is summarized with a synopsis, followed by a content outline and lists of key elements including characters, places, and concepts. This supplement is useful when reading the Bible itself.

Meyers, Carol. *ReDiscovering Eve: Ancient Israelite Women in Context*. Oxford: Oxford University Press, 2013.

ReDiscovering Eve places the Hebrew Bible within its wider historical context to appreciate the integral and critical roles of everyday women in the ancient Near East. Dr. Meyers demonstrates how the elite male writers of the Bible skew our understanding of the biblical world. This distorted view can be balanced by archaeological evidence that helps unearth discoveries about women's importance in antiquity.

Meyers, Carol, Toni Craven, and Ross S. Kraemer, eds. *Women in Scripture: A Dictionary of Named and Unnamed Women in the Hebrew Bible, the Apocryphal/Deuterocanonical Books, and the New Testament*. New York: Houghton Mifflin, 2000.

A few introductory essays provide a brief, helpful background, followed by short essays on every woman, girl, and goddess in the Bible. Part 1 gives entries of named women (in alphabetical order) followed by unnamed women (part 2; noted by chapter and verses in canonical order). Part 3 comprises essays on female deities and personifications. This book is a useful reference tool for an overview of any female biblical character.

Newsom, Carol A., Sharon H. Ringe, and Jacqueline E. Lapsley, eds. *Women's Bible Commentary*, 3rd ed. Louisville: Westminster John Knox, 2012.

This valuable volume provides a chapter on every book of the Bible and Apocrypha. Each essay begins with a discussion of the biblical book to provide context, then focuses on women characters or issues related to women's lives. A few supplementary essays review the history of interpretation around select biblical women. (I pull this book from my shelf frequently.)

Reid, Barbara E., et al., eds. Wisdom Commentary Series. 60 vols. planned, 28 available. St. Louis: Chalice, 2015–.

This new biblical commentary series provides in-depth discussion of every book of the Bible from a feminist perspective. Scholars come from a wide range of backgrounds, and each volume includes writings from multiple contributors, ensuring diversity of voices. Issues of translation are also incorporated into each book. These commentaries are a terrific resource for in-depth study of a particular biblical book and may be especially helpful for preachers and seminarians.

Smith, Mitzi J. and Jin Young Choi, eds. *Minoritized Women Reading Race and Ethnicity: Intersectional Approaches to Constructed Identity and Early Christian Texts*. Washington, DC: Lexington Books, 2020.

Like the volume on the Hebrew Bible edited by Gale Yee (below), this book on the New Testament and early Christian texts brings together scholars from different backgrounds (here African American, Asian American, and Asian women). They read with attention to race, class, and other aspects of social location to unmask unspoken underlying assumptions of whiteness as normative.

Stol, Marten. *Women in the Ancient Near East.* Translated by Helen Richardson and Mervyn Richardson. Berlin: de Gruyter, 2016.

This hefty volume offers broad knowledge of women's lives in the ancient Near East. While focused on Mesopotamia and not on the Bible specifically, it still provides context and comparative information for understanding women's lives in this region of the ancient world. Remarkably, this book is open access and, therefore, free. If you type the title into a browser and then click on the open access link, you can download the entire book (all 708 pages!).

Trible, Phyllis. *Texts of Terror: Literary-Feminist Readings of Biblical Narratives.* 40th anniv. ed. Minneapolis: Fortress, 2022.

Dr. Trible established feminist biblical interpretation of the Old Testament. Her first book, *God and the Rhetoric of Sexuality* (Minneapolis: Fortress, 1978), offers close literary readings of biblical texts to rediscover stories of women and to unmask misogynist biases in common interpretations. *Texts of Terror*, first published in 1984 and now reprinted in a fortieth anniversary edition, unflinchingly examines the sad stories of Hagar, Tamar, the Levite's concubine, and Jephthah's daughter to reveal their painful, poignant power. The phrase "texts of terror" has entered the lexicon of biblical studies as this book is an essential classic.

Yee, Gale A., ed. *The Hebrew Bible: Feminist and Intersectional Perspectives*. Minneapolis: Fortress, 2018.

This book begins with a brief history of feminist biblical scholarship, noting how dynamics of race and class have often been ignored in discussions of gender. In the introduction, Dr. Yee urges readers to approach the Bible intersectionally, with awareness of how multiple vectors of identity converge in biblical characters (as in living people). Four subsequent essays by feminist and womanist scholars explore the Torah/Pentateuch, the Deuteronomistic History, the Prophetic Books, and the Writings to nuance and enrich understandings of texts related to women.

Acknowledgments

As my students know, my favorite word in the Bible is *pele* (פלא), a Hebrew term designating that which is difficult and that which is wonderful. Same word. Think about it: most anything worthwhile in life—like learning and getting an education, forming meaningful relationships, raising children, or developing a career—is both difficult and wonderful. Writing this book has been *pele*.

A difficult part has been getting up at 5:30 most mornings for the past year and a half to write for a few hours before the rest of my workday started. (Shout-out to coffee—which definitely deserves an acknowledgement!)

But a wonderful part has been collaborating with others as this book took shape.

I would like to thank Ansel Elkins for sharing her Edenic poem, "Autobiography of Eve," to be reprinted in this book.

The team at Baker Academic has been a writer's dream. Jim Kinney supported and guided this project from its earliest beginning and remained attentive and helpful at every step of the process. Melisa Blok, Anna English, and Dustyn Keepers have also worked hard on this book sharing valuable expertise with thoughtfulness and grace. I am honored to work with such an outstanding publisher.

I wrote part of this book while on sabbatical and living in Paris with my husband, Bill. I am grateful to General Theological Seminary for this sabbatical. I would also like to thank the Conant Foundation of the Episcopal Church for a grant that enabled me to write and research while abroad. Bill and I were hosted by kind and generous French friends: Yves-Laurent, Sophie, Camille, and Maëlle Le Berre; and most especially the Rigaudière family: Claire, Nicolas, Aurélien, Élise, Grégoire, Victor, and Ombeline, who opened their home to us and treated us like family.

Two writers who live on General's campus are renowned authors; both were gracious and helpful. Jonathan Merritt met with me when I was starting to write this book and gave terrific advice for its development. Shauna Niequist has been unwaveringly encouraging, reflecting the huge heart that her hundreds of thousands of readers know she has. I am grateful to both.

Two of my students, Adelia Nunn and Neal Medlyn, helped with research and proofing chapters. I would like to thank them, and especially to thank Neal for his close attention to the manuscript in its final stages.

Friends, family, students, and colleagues have also shared their stories, offered insights, and read over sections of this book to give feedback. For these precious gifts of time, attention, and permission, I would like to thank Lawrence Bartley, Chris Barton, Kathi Boland, Keith Brewer, Anne Burns, Joshua Bruner, Kimberly George, Dan Gutman, Jeremy Hollingshead, Alexandra LeClere, Kyong-Jin Lee, Susan Leet, John Martens, Rochelle Melander, Doug Mohrmann, Jeehei Park, Kate Parker-Burgard, Valerie Parker, Kim Peterson, Elizabeth Schrader Polczer, Mary Ann Schoenberger, Amy Steinberg, Eric Thomas, Wendy Weiner, and Alice Yafeh-Deigh. I'd like to add a special thank-you to Leslie Thayer Piper—cherished friend and gifted editor—who offered excellent suggestions for polishing this manuscript.

Finally—and most importantly—with a heart full of love, I thank my husband, Bill, and our grown children, Graham and Mari. Not only have they read over chapters and given permission to share personal stories in these pages, but they share the intimacies of their lives with me, and I with them. I dedicated the published version of my dissertation to Bill, but I have not published a subsequent book that I thought worthy of a dedication to Graham and Mari, until this one. Even if it does nothing else, this book will stand as a testimony to the love of this mother for her children. And for that, I am grateful beyond words.

Abbreviations

General

BCE	before common era	masc.	masculine
CE	common era	MT	Masoretic Text
cf.	compare (Latin: *confer*)	v.	verse
fem.	feminine	vv.	verses

Bible Books

Old Testament

Gen.	Genesis	Song	Song of Songs
Exod.	Exodus	Isa.	Isaiah
Lev.	Leviticus	Jer.	Jeremiah
Num.	Numbers	Lam.	Lamentations
Deut.	Deuteronomy	Ezek.	Ezekiel
Josh.	Joshua	Dan.	Daniel
Judg.	Judges	Hosea	Hosea
Ruth	Ruth	Joel	Joel
1–2 Sam.	1–2 Samuel	Amos	Amos
1–2 Kings	1–2 Kings	Obad.	Obadiah
1–2 Chron.	1–2 Chronicles	Jon.	Jonah
Ezra	Ezra	Mic.	Micah
Neh.	Nehemiah	Nah.	Nahum
Esther	Esther	Hab.	Habakkuk
Job	Job	Zeph.	Zephaniah
Ps(s).	Psalm(s)	Hag.	Haggai
Prov.	Proverbs	Zech.	Zechariah
Eccles.	Ecclesiastes	Mal.	Malachi

New Testament

Matt.	Matthew	1–2 Thess.	1–2 Thessalonians
Mark	Mark	1–2 Tim.	1–2 Timothy
Luke	Luke	Titus	Titus
John	John	Philem.	Philemon
Acts	Acts	Heb.	Hebrews
Rom.	Romans	James	James
1–2 Cor.	1–2 Corinthians	1–2 Pet.	1–2 Peter
Gal.	Galatians	1–3 John	1–3 John
Eph.	Ephesians	Jude	Jude
Phil.	Philippians	Rev.	Revelation
Col.	Colossians		

Bible Versions

ESV	English Standard Version		*Translation according to*
KJV	King James Version		*the Traditional Hebrew*
MSG	The Message		*Text*
NABRE	New American Bible, Revised Edition	NKJV	New King James Version
		NLT	New Living Translation
NASB	New American Standard Bible	NRSV	New Revised Standard Version
NA²⁸	*Novum Testamentum Graece*, Nestle-Aland, 28th ed.	NRSVUE	New Revised Standard Version Updated Edition
		RSV	Revised Standard Version
NIV	New International Version	RSVCE	Revised Standard Version Catholic Edition
NJB	New Jerusalem Bible		
NJPS	*The Tanakh: The Holy Scriptures: The New JPS*		

Bibliography

Abbott-Smith, George. *A Manual Lexicon of the New Testament.* 3rd ed. 1921. Reprint, Edinburgh: T&T Clark, 1981.

Ackerman, Susan. "Asherah/Asherim." In Meyers, Craven, and Kraemer, *Women in Scripture*, 508–11.

———. "Asherah, the West Semitic Goddess of Spinning and Weaving?" *Journal of Near Eastern Studies* 67, no. 1 (2008): 1–29.

———. *Women and the Religion of Ancient Israel.* New Haven: Yale University Press, 2022.

American Psychiatric Association. *Diagnostic and Statistical Manual of Mental Disorders DSM- V.* Washington, DC: American Psychiatric Press, 2013.

Archer, Aundray Jermaine. "Not Sneaky but Smart: Sagacity from the Speaking Snake." In *My So-Called Biblical Life: Imagined Stories from the World's Best-Selling Book*, edited by Julie Faith Parker, 1–11. Eugene, OR: Wipf & Stock, 2017.

Barr, Jane. "The Vulgate Genesis and St. Jerome's Attitude to Women." In *Papers Presented to the Eighth International Conference on Patristic Studies Held at Oxford, 1979*, edited by Elizabeth A. Livingstone, 268–73. Studia Patristica 17. Oxford: Pergamon, 1982.

Bartley, Lawrence. "I Am Not Your Inmate." *The Marshall Project Language Project.* https://www.themarshallproject.org/2021/04/12/i-am-not-your -inmate.

Betsworth, Sharon, and Julie Faith Parker. "'Where Have All the Young Girls Gone?' Discovering the Girls of the Bible through Childist Analysis of Exodus 2 and Mark 5–7." *Journal of Feminist Studies in Religion* 38, no. 2 (2022): 125–41.

Boff, Leonardo. *Ecclesiogenesis: The Base Communities Reinvent the Church.* Translated by Robert R. Barr. Maryknoll, NY: Orbis Books, 1986.

Brown, Francis, S. R. Driver, and Charles A. Briggs. *A Hebrew and English Lexicon of the Old Testament.* Peabody, MA: Hendrickson, 1999.

Butler, Judith. *Gender Trouble: Feminism and the Subversion of Identity.* 2nd ed. New York: Routledge, 2007.

Carroll, John B., ed. *Language, Thought, and Reality: Selected Writings of Benjamin Lee Whorf.* Cambridge, MA: MIT Press, 1956.

Coogan, Michael D., and Mark S. Smith, trans. and ed. *Stories from Ancient Canaan.* 2nd ed. Louisville: Westminster John Knox, 2012.

Crawford, Mari, and Taha Rakla. "One Flew over the Cuckoo's Nest." March 30, 2022. In *Beautiful Bipolar Badass,* podcast, MP3 audio, 49:08. https://open.spotify.com/episode/1eqOyPzPkqE6oijyTbmOVc.

———. "What Is Bipolar Disorder Part 1." March 30, 2022. In *Beautiful Bipolar Badass,* podcast, MP3 audio, 33:26. https://open.spotify.com/episode/0SvUT1OPRFUqFIlAnD5Na6.

Creach, Jerome F. D. *Discovering Psalms: Content, Interpretation, Reception.* Discovering Biblical Texts. Grand Rapids: Eerdmans, 2020.

deClaissé-Walford, S. G. "Ishmael, the Quran, and the Bible." *Acta Theologica* 39 (2019):148–64.

Dever, William G. *Did God Have a Wife? Archaeology and Folk Religion in Ancient Israel.* Grand Rapids: Eerdmans, 2008.

Dietrich, Manfried, Oswald Loretz, and Joaquín Sanmartín, eds. *KTU [Keilalphabetische Texte aus Ugarit]: The Cuneiform Alphabetic Texts from Ugarit, Ras Ibn Hani, and Other Places.* 3rd. enlarged ed. Munster: Ugarit-Verlag, 2013.

Duncan, Celena M. "The Book of Ruth: On Boundaries, Love, and Truth." In Goss and West, *Take Back the Word,* 92–102.

Eng, Milton. *The Days of Our Years: A Lexical Semantic Study of the Life Cycle in Biblical Israel.* Library of Hebrew Bible/Old Testament Studies 464. London: T&T Clark, 2011.

Gafney, Wilda. *Daughters of Miriam: Women Prophets in Ancient Israel.* Minneapolis: Fortress, 2008.

Garroway, Kristine Henriksen. *Growing Up in Ancient Israel: Children in Material Culture in Biblical Times*. Archaeology and Biblical Studies 23. Atlanta: SBL Press, 2018.

Gergis, Sonia. "The Power of Women Musicians in the Ancient Near East: The Roots of Prejudice." *British Journal of Music Education* 10, no. 3 (1993): 189–96.

Goss, Robert E., and Mona West, eds. *Take Back the Word: A Queer Reading of the Bible*. Cleveland: Pilgrim, 2000.

Graves-Brown, Carolyn. *Dancing for Hathor: Women in Ancient Egypt*. London: Continuum, 2010.

Gunkel, Hermann. Completed by Joachim Begrich. *Introduction to Psalms: The Genres of the Religious Lyric of Israel*. Translated by James D. Nogalski. Macon, GA: Mercer University Press, 1998. Originally published in 1933.

Helsel, Carolyn B., and Song-Mi Suzie Park. *The Flawed Family of God: Stories about the Imperfect Families of Genesis*. Louisville: Westminster John Knox, 2021.

Henderson, Timothy P. *The Gospel of Peter and Early Christian Apologetics: Rewriting the Story of Jesus' Death, Burial, and Resurrection*. Tübingen: Mohr Siebeck, 2011.

Hornsby, Teresa J., and Deryn Guest. *Transgender, Intersex, and Biblical Interpretation*. Semeia Studies 83. Atlanta: SBL Press, 2016.

Jansen, Katherine Ludwig. *The Making of the Magdalen: Preaching and Popular Devotion in the Later Middle Ages*. Princeton: Princeton University Press, 2000.

Jastrow, Marcus. *A Dictionary of the Targumim, Talmud Babli and Yerushalami, and the Midrashic Literature*. London: Trübner & Co., 1886. Reprint, New York: Judaica Press, 1971.

King, Karen L. "Canonization and Marginalization: Mary of Magdala." In *The Postcolonial Biblical Reader*, edited by R. S. Sugirtharajah, 284–90. Malden, MA: Blackwell, 2006.

———. *The Gospel of Mary of Magdala: Jesus and the First Woman Apostle*. Santa Rosa, CA: Polebridge, 2003.

Knowles, Melody D. "Feminist Interpretation of the Psalms." In *The Oxford Handbook of the Psalms*, edited by William P. Brown, 424–36. New York: Oxford University Press, 2014.

Knust, Jennifer Wright. *Unprotected Texts: The Bible's Surprising Contradictions about Sex and Desire.* New York: Harper Collins, 2011.

Koehler, Ludwig, Walter Baumgartner, and Johann J. Stamm. *The Hebrew and Aramaic Lexicon of the Old Testament.* Study Edition. Translated and edited under the supervision of Mervyn E. J. Richardson. 2 vols. Leiden: Brill, 2001.

Kramer, Heinrich, and Jacob Springer. *Malleus Maleficarum.* Speyer, Germany: Peter Drach, 1486. https://www.sacred-texts.com/pag/mm/index.htm.

Levine, Samuel J. *Was Yosef on the Spectrum? Understanding Joseph through Torah, Midrash, and Classical Jewish Sources.* Jerusalem: Urim, 2018.

Lewis, David M. "Classical and Near Eastern Slavery in the First Millennium BCE." In *The Oxford Handbook of Greek and Roman Slaveries*, edited by Stephen Hodkinson, Marc Kleijwegt, and Kostas Vlassopoulos, 1–22. Oxford: Oxford University Press, 2018. https://doi.org/10.1093/oxfordhb/9780199575251.013.42.

Lion, Brigitte. "Literacy and Gender." In *The Oxford Handbook of Cuneiform Culture*, edited by Karen Radner and Eleanor Robson, 90–112. Oxford: Oxford University Press, 2011.

Marchal, Joseph A. "LGBTIQ Strategies of Interpretation." In *The Oxford Handbook of New Testament, Gender, and Sexuality*, edited by Benjamin H. Dunning, 177–95. New York: Oxford University Press, 2019.

Marsman, Hennie J. *Women in Ugarit and Israel: Their Social & Religious Position in the Context of the Ancient Near East.* Oudtestamentische Studiën 49. Leiden: Brill, 2003.

Martin, Colby. *UnClobber: Rethinking Our Misuse of the Bible on Homosexuality.* Louisville: Westminster John Knox, 2016.

Mato Nunpa, Chris. *The Great Evil (Wosice Tanka Kin): Christianity, the Bible, and the Native American Genocide.* Tucson: See Sharp, 2020.

———. "A Sweet-Smelling Sacrifice: Genocide, the Bible, and the Indigenous Peoples of the United States, Selected Examples." In *Confronting Genocide: Judaism, Christianity, Islam*, edited by Steven Leonard Jacobs, 47–63. Lanham, MD: Lexington Books, 2008.

Meyers, Carol L. "Naamah 1." In Meyers, Craven, and Kraemer, *Women in Scripture*, 129.

———. "Of Drums and Damsels: Women's Performance in Ancient Israel." *The Biblical Archaeologist* 54, no. 1 (1991): 16–27.

———. "Rebekah." In Meyers, Craven, and Kraemer, *Women in Scripture*, 143–45.

———. *Re-Discovering Eve: Ancient Israelite Women in Context*. New York: Oxford University Press, 2013.

———. "Was Ancient Israel a Patriarchal Society?" *Journal of Biblical Literature* 133, no. 1 (2014): 8–27.

———. "Women with Hand-Drums, Dancing." In Meyers, Craven, and Kraemer, *Women in Scripture*, 189–91.

Meyers, Carol, Toni Craven, and Ross S. Kraemer, eds. *Women in Scripture: A Dictionary of Named and Unnamed Women in the Hebrew Bible, the Apocryphal/Deuterocanonical Books, and the New Testament*. Boston: Houghton Mifflin, 2000.

Moss, Candida. "A Conspiracy to Suppress Mary Magdalene? No Longer Just a Dan Brown Plotline." *Daily Beast*, July 21, 2018. https://www.the dailybeast.com/a-conspiracy-to-suppress-mary-magdalene-no-longer-just -a-dan-brown-plotline.

Newsom, Carol A. *The Book of Job: A Contest of Moral Imaginations*. New York: Oxford University Press, 2003.

———. "Job." In Newsom, Ringe, and Lapsley, *Women's Bible Commentary*, 208–15.

Newsom, Carol A., and Sharon H. Ringe, eds. *Women's Bible Commentary*. 2nd ed. Louisville: Westminster John Knox, 1998.

Newsom, Carol A., Sharon H. Ringe, and Jacqueline E. Lapsley, eds. *Women's Bible Commentary*. 3rd ed. Louisville: Westminster John Knox, 2012.

Niditch, Susan. "Prophetic Dreams and Visions in the Hebrew Bible." *Bible Odyssey*. https://www.bibleodyssey.org:443/passages/related-articles /prophetic-dreams-and-visions-in-the-hebrew-bible.

Nissinen, Martti. *Ancient Prophecy: Near Eastern, Biblical, and Greek Perspectives*. Oxford: Oxford University Press, 2017.

O'Day, Gail. "Martha." In Meyers, Craven, and Kraemer, *Women in Scripture*, 114–16.

Osiek, Carolyn. "Household Codes." *Bible Odyssey*. https://www.bible odyssey.org:443/people/related-articles/household-codes.

———. "Mary 3." In Meyers, Craven, and Kraemer, *Women in Scripture*, 120–23.

Parker, Julie Faith. "Blaming Eve Alone: Translation, Omission, and Implications of עמה in Genesis 3:6b." *Journal of Biblical Literature* 132, no. 4 (2013): 729–47.

———. "Call Them Ishmael: A Childist Investigation of Israel's First Son as a Powerful Precedent." In *A Sage in New Haven: Essays on the Prophets, the Writings, and the Ancient World in Honor of Robert R. Wilson*, edited by Alison Acker Gruseke and Carolyn J. Sharp, 285–95. Ägypten und Altes Testament 117. Münster: Zaphon, 2023.

———. "Children in the Hebrew Bible and Childist Interpretation." *Currents in Biblical Research* 17, no. 2 (2019): 130–57.

———. "Engaging Studies of Children in the Bible: What Is Going On and Why You Should Care." *Children & Society* (2022):1–15. https://doi.org/10.1111/chso.12645.

———. *Valuable and Vulnerable*: *Children in the Hebrew Bible, Especially the Elisha Cycle*. Brown Judaic Studies 355. Providence: Brown University, 2013.

———. "Women Warriors and Devoted Daughters: The Powerful Young Woman in Ugaritic Narrative Poetry." *Ugarit-Forschungen* 38 (2006): 557–75.

Perkins, Benjamin. "Coming Out, Lazarus's and Ours: Queer Reflections of a Psychospiritual, Political Journey." In Goss and West, *Take Back the Word*, 196–205.

Phipps, William. *Genesis and Gender: Biblical Myths of Sexuality and Their Cultural Impact*. New York: Praeger, 1989.

Pogrebin, Letty Cottin. "Gloria Steinem." In *The Shalvi/Hyman Encyclopedia of Jewish Women*. Jewish Women's Archive. March 20, 2009. https://jwa.org/encyclopedia/article/steinem-gloria.

Riley, Sara K. "The Hand Drum (תף) and Israelite Women's Musical Tradition." *Studia Antiqua* 13, no. 1 (2014): 23–47.

Rowlett, Lori L. "Disney's Pocahontas and Joshua's Rahab in Postcolonial Perspective." In *Culture, Entertainment, and the Bible*, edited by George Aichele, 66–75. Journal for the Study of the Old Testament: Supplement Series 309. Sheffield: Sheffield Academic Press, 2000.

Sawyer, Wendy. "How Much Do Incarcerated People Earn in Each State?" *Prison Policy Initiative*, April 10, 2017. https://www.prisonpolicy.org/blog/2017/04/10/wages/.

Schaberg, Jane. "Luke." In Newsom and Ringe, *Women's Bible Commentary*, 363–80.

Schaberg, Jane, and Sharon H. Ringe. "Luke." In Newsom, Ringe, and Lapsley, *Women's Bible Commentary*, 493–511.

Schmitt, Rüdiger. "Astarte, Mistress of Horses, Lady of the Chariot: The Warrior Aspect of Astarte." *Die Welt des Orients* 43, no. 2 (2013): 213–25.

Schrader, Elizabeth. "Was Martha of Bethany Added to the Fourth Gospel in the Second Century?" *Harvard Theological Review* 110, no. 3 (2017): 360–92.

Schrader, Elizabeth, and Joan E. Taylor. "The Meaning of 'Magdalene': A Review of Literary Evidence." *Journal of Biblical Literature* 140, no. 4 (2021): 751–73.

Schüssler Fiorenza, Elisabeth. *In Memory of Her: A Feminist Theological Reconstruction of Christian Origins*. New York: Crossroad, 1983.

———. *Wo/men, Scripture, and Politics: Exploring the Cultural Imprint of the Bible*. Eugene, OR: Cascade Books, 2021.

Seow, C. L. *Job 1–21: Interpretation and Commentary*. Illuminations. Grand Rapids: Eerdmans, 2013.

———. "Job's Wife." In *Engaging the Bible in a Gendered World*, edited by Linda Day and Carolyn Pressler, 141–50. Louisville: Westminster John Knox, 2006.

Shimron, Yonat. "Scribes Tried to Blot Her Out. Now a Scholar Is Trying to Recover the Real Mary Magdalene." *Religion News Service*, July 19, 2019. https://religionnews.com/2019/07/19/scribes-tried-to-blot-her-out-now-a-scholar-is-trying-to-recover-the-real-mary-magdalene/.

———. "Was Mary Magdalene Really from Magdala? Two Scholars Examine the Evidence." *National Catholic Reporter*, January 11, 2022. Reprinted in the *Christian Century*, January 24, 2022. https://www.ncronline.org/news/people/was-mary-magdalene-really-magdala-two-scholars-examine-evidence.

Snell, Daniel C. *Life in the Ancient Near East*. New Haven: Yale University Press, 1997.

Steinem, Gloria. "A New Egalitarian Lifestyle." *New York Times*, August 26, 1971.

Stökl, Jonathan. "Deborah, Huldah, and Innibana: Constructions of Hebrew Prophecy in the Ancient Near East and the Hebrew Bible." *Journal of Ancient Judaism* 6, no. 3 (2015): 320–34.

Stökl, Jonathan, and Corrine L. Carvalho, eds. *Prophets Male and Female: Gender and Prophecy in the Hebrew Bible, the Eastern Mediterranean, and the Ancient Near East*. Ancient Israel and Its Literature 15. Atlanta: SBL Press, 2013.

Stol, Marten. *Women in the Ancient Near East*. Translated by Helen and Mervyn Richardson. Berlin: de Gruyter, 2016.

Stone, Ken. "1 and 2 Samuel." In *The Queer Bible Commentary*, edited by Deryn Guest, Robert E. Goss, Mona West, and Thomas Bohache, 195–221. London: SCM, 2006.

Strudwick, Helen, ed. *The Encyclopedia of Ancient Egypt*. London: Amber, 2006.

Tamber-Rosenau, Caryn. "A Queer Critique of Looking for 'Male' and 'Female' Voices in the Hebrew Bible." In *The Oxford Handbook of Feminist Approaches to the Hebrew Bible*, edited by Susanne Scholz, 479–93. New York: Oxford University Press, 2021.

Tamez, Elsa. "Religión, género y violencia." *Agenda Latinoamericana* (2011): 154–55.

Travis, Irene S. "Love Your Mother: A Lesbian Womanist Reading of Scripture." In Goss and West, *Take Back the Word*, 35–42.

Trible, Phyllis. *God and the Rhetoric of Sexuality*. Philadelphia: Fortress, 1978.

———. *Texts of Terror: Literary-Feminist Readings of Biblical Narratives*. Philadelphia: Fortress, 1984.

Tyldesley, Joyce. *Daughters of Isis: Women of Ancient Egypt*. New York: Penguin, 1995.

Valentine, Katy E. "Reading the Slave Girl of Acts 16:16–18 in Light of Enslavement and Disability." *Biblical Interpretation* 26, no. 3 (2018): 352–68.

van der Toorn, Karel, Bob Becking, and Pieter W. van der Horst, eds. *The Dictionary of Deities and Demons in the Bible*. Leiden: Brill, 1999. 2nd rev. ed. Grand Rapids: Eerdmans, 1999.

Van Harn, Roger E., and Brent A. Strawn, eds. *Psalms for Preaching and Worship: A Lectionary Commentary*. Grand Rapids: Eerdmans, 2009.

Vines, Matthew. *God and the Gay Christian: The Biblical Case in Support of Same-Sex Relationships*. New York: Convergent, 2014.

Weems, Renita J. *Just a Sister Away: A Womanist Vision of Women's Relationships in the Bible*. Philadelphia: Innisfree, 1988.

Yafeh-Deigh, Alice. "Children, Motherhood, and the Social Death of the Childless Woman: The Social and Theological Construction of Infertility in the Hebrew Bible and in Cameroon." *Biblical Interpretation* 28, no. 5 (2020): 606–34.

Yamauchi, Edwin M., and Marvin R. Wilson. "Childbirth and Children." In *Dictionary of Daily Life in Biblical and Post-Biblical Antiquity*, 1:280–89. Peabody, MA: Hendrickson, 2014.

Yee, Gale A., ed. *The Hebrew Bible: Feminist and Intersectional Perspectives*. Minneapolis: Fortress, 2018.

———. "Thinking Intersectionally: Gender, Race, Class, and the Etceteras of Our Discipline." *Journal of Biblical Literature* 139, no. 1 (2020): 7–26.

Scripture Index

Subject Index